MW00788361

TEN PERCENT OF the profits from this book will be donated equally to three different African American Baptist churches in Connecticut.

I would like to express my deep gratitude to Reverend Tommie Jackson, Dr. Boise Kimber, and Dr. Joseph Ford—all present and past leaders of Faith Tabernacle Missionary Baptist Church, along with the members of Faith Tabernacle, for the willingness to have me worship alongside them and to share their vibrant Christian faith with me.

The message of "Life, Love, Liberty," as found in the weekly worship bulletin for the sermon has been an inspiration and eye-opener. It was so inspirational that it motivated me to run for governor of the state of Connecticut in 2017–2018. In time, it has become the five L's of life, love, liberty, listen, and learn. Rev. Tommie Jackson was the minister at Faith Tabernacle and was instrumental in adopting life, love, and liberty for the bulletin. Dr. Boise Kimber served as the interim pastor after Rev. Tommie Jackson left. Dr. Kimber was gracious enough to meet with me for countless Thursdays to go over the policies and platforms of my campaign for governorship. Dr. Joseph Ford became the full-time minister of Faith Tabernacle in 2019, and he too has listened to me and advised me as I proposed policy changes after the killing of George Floyd and Breonna Taylor in the spring of 2020.

I am grateful for the generosity of each of these ministers for their positive message and for their patience to sit with me. Ralph; Betty; Emma; Leon; Deacons Brevard, Dupree, McClintock, Elliott, Homer and the late Jack Bryant have all extended a warm hand of fellowship. To the leadership of President Guy Fortt and my fellow executive committee members of the Stamford, NAACP, I also express my gratitude for allowing me to participate, and sharing your feedback. And so my education continues.

I would acknowledge the many Democrats who have also been willing to sit with me and offer feedback and refinements, but the intolerance of the intolerants and cancel cancer is so great that they may suffer a backlash from the intolerants if identified by name. Nonetheless, I thank you for your generosity of time and insight.

The
SCHOOL-*to*-PRISON
PIPELINE

How the Public School Monopoly and the Teachers'
Unions Deny School Choice to High-Needs Black,
Hispanic, White, Asian, and Other Students

PETER THALHEIM

Fulton Books, Inc.
Meadville, PA

Fulton Books
Meadville, PA

Published by Fulton Books 2022

ISBN 978-1-64952-995-4 (paperback)
ISBN 978-1-64952-996-1 (digital)

Printed in the United States of America

Contents

Introduction

WHO WOULD THINK that there is a school-to-prison pipe-line? It is certainly not a concept that was in my mind before I ran for governor of the State of Connecticut in 2017 to 2018. As a public school student from kindergarten through twelfth grade, school was part of the continuum of growing up and making a life for yourself in America. First there was preschool at First Congregational Church from the fall of 1964 to 1965 for half days. We had immigrated in May 1963, when I was just turning three, and I started talking later than most. Since we were from Germany, we spoke German in the house, which over time became a combination of English and German. A sentence might start in one language and finish in another. Needless to say, I could not speak much English by the time I started preschool after sixteen months in the United States. My mother told me that I absolutely idolized my preschool teacher. My preschool teacher, on the other hand, thought I was a little stupid. If she told us to do stuff or asked me to do something, I wouldn't necessarily understand because I couldn't speak English yet. Then on to kindergarten at the Old Greenwich Elementary School, built in 1902. It was a grand building with tall ceilings. The tall ceilings helped handle the hot weather in June and September as there was no air-conditioning. There were windows above the doors so that the door could be closed, but air could still circulate between open windows and the hall. If things got too hot in September or June, the janitors would bring out strong fans on tall metal poles to move the air around. Everyone sweated, but that is how it was.

The same practical ceramic tiles still adorn the hallways at the OG Elementary School today. That is the benefit of choosing durable, quality ingredients for a public building decades ago. They are a very practical material as it can take fingerprints and minor collisions from carts and movie projectors. In these same halls, we would do air raid drills in in the late 1960s. The teachers did not tell us exactly why the whole school would crouch in the hallways, away from the windows with our heads tucked between our knees. But in proper civil defense mode, you had to do something to prepare for the unimaginable Armageddon of nuclear annihilation in a nuclear showdown between the Soviet Union and the United States. The Cuban Missile Crisis under President Kennedy had only occurred in October 1962, perhaps the closest we have come to nuclear war since World War II. That was only two years previous to 1964. There were signs on stout public buildings in yellow and black: Fallout Shelter. The sign was three yellow triangles over a black circle. That would let you know where you could go to try to survive the nuclear hurricane force winds from the explosions and then the subsequent radioactive fallout. Was it realistic that this would save you? Probably not, but a subway station in the city would probably be one of the better spots, albeit at ground zero of a Soviet missile strike. Fortunately, we don't do these drills anymore. Instead there are lockdown drills in the event one or more nutjobs with a gun or other weapon attacks an individual school.

Back when I went to school, elementary school went K–6, and then the nearby Eastern Junior High School went 7–9, and then Greenwich High School was 10–12. I was proud to be part of the largest graduating class from Greenwich High School in 1978 of about 950 students. Today it is about 650 students in the senior class. I just like to remind my kids that things were tougher then but at the same time better then. Wink, wink. Now after high school, for many of us in a well-to-do community, was the progression to college, and by age fourteen, I had already decided that I wanted to study law and become an attorney as both my grandfathers had been attorneys, although neither of my parents went to college owing to the dislocation of World War II. I was also interested in politics as a great number of politicians in America were also attorneys. There had to be some reason for that. That meant that as I was working through high school, I assumed that I would do four years of college and then another three years of law school. That is a lot of school after graduating from high school. Nowhere did a school-to-prison pipeline show up in my plans.

When the United States of America declared its independence from Great Britain in 1776, New England, the colonies of Connecticut, Massachusetts, Rhode Island, Maine, and New Hampshire, with Vermont to become the fourteenth state soon after in 1791, were the most literate places on the earth. The colonists believed education key to a free society. Literacy ran from 85 to 90 percent for men, excluding slaves. The southern slaveholding states, on the other hand, had capital punishment in place for teaching slaves to read or write. *See* W. E. B. DuBois and Frederick Douglass recitations. The literacy rate in Great Britain and France was not even half the literacy rate in New England. And who supported the literacy of New Englanders then? The churches. In Connecticut, a town couldn't be chartered if it didn't have a church. My church, the First Congregational Church of Old Greenwich, was granted its charter in 1640, and thereby Greenwich could begin as a town. Churches were instrumental in New England to educate her citizenry. Today, we have the state running most of our K-12 education. There are also private schools, public charter schools (a form of public school run on public dollars and some private funding), religious schools like catholic schools, or yeshivas for Jewish students. We even homeschool our children. And more recently, there has been the advent of online schooling. Who knew that online schooling would come in handy after the outbreak of the COVID-19 coronavirus to differing levels of success? But for the majority of students, nothing takes the place of in-person teaching and being with your peers in school.

So where does the school-to-prison pipeline come in? The traditional view of the school-to-prison pipeline is rather narrow. Wikipedia put the pipeline as follows: "A disturbing national trend wherein children are funneled out of public schools and into the juvenile and criminal justice systems. Many of these children have learning disabilities or histories of poverty, abuse, or neglect, and would benefit from additional educational and counseling services. Instead, they are isolated, punished, and pushed out."[1]

The Wikipedia article continues that the pipeline is a "disproportionate tendency of minors and young adults from disadvantaged backgrounds incarcerated because of increasingly harsh school and municipal policies."[2] The amount of children that were disciplined was focused on school disturbances, with some communities having "zero-tolerance" for disturbing behavior and the increase of having police in school, made the schools more readily bringing potential violations of laws to the attention of the school police officers. The American Civil Liberties Union, also known as the ACLU, called these policies a disaster on their website: "While cops in school lead to students being criminalized for behavior that should be handled inside school." The ACLU is "working to challenge numerous policies and practices within *public* school systems and the juvenile justice system that contribute to the school-to-prison pipeline."[3] Nowhere does the ACLU cite that they are going to address a root of the problem: the lack of family formation. Children of households with two parents or guardians are statistically less disruptive than those from single-parent households. Doctors say that prevention is the best medicine. To ignore the most basic cure is to miss the mark. Wouldn't public policy be better if it aimed to increase two-parent households and thereby reduce students who might be more disruptive to their classmates and at the same time foster children at greater

---

[1]   "School to Prison Pipeline," July 30, 2019, wikipedia.com.

[2]   Id.

[3]   aclu.org, July 30, 2019.

ease with themselves and their peers? Clearly this would not be the only policy but one of many to help the chances of our children and young adults work toward realizing their potential. And you need the proper morals and values to achieve your full potential as an adult.

It is inaccurate to charge school administrators who try to preserve the educational opportunities for all students in the school by creating a safe environment so that students can learn with creating a school-to-prison pipeline. Can we ignore a root cause and still hope to lower the suspension numbers regardless of its negative impact on classmates?

Or do the statists keep the pipeline open to ensure that as many students stay in the school-to-prison pipeline as possible versus taking them out of the pipeline and allowing them to go to public charters or private schools via vouchers? The state "wins" by keeping more people in the state-run pipeline. The public unions "win" by the union keeping more unionized school staff and keeping the dues gravy train coming in to support public unions, who in turn use their political strength to help elect candidates who favor unionized public schools versus school choice for our children and young people. This is a win for the National Education Association and the American Federation of Teachers, the two leading unions for public school teachers. But is keeping the pipeline open a win for our students? How do the children win if their educational options are artificially restricted? The students lose by being blocked in sometimes failing public schools with no viable choice to go elsewhere. And the poorer you are, the fewer choices you generally have. This denial of school choice would particularly impact black students, as blacks have disproportionately less money than the average American. In fact, the average African-American has one-tenth of the net worth than the average white American. Although the average age of an African American is less than that of the average white, the wealth disparity is extreme. How to fix that disparity is for another book, but suffice it to say that with less wealth, African Americans have fewer educational options for their children. That is something that can be addressed, and this book tries to do just that.

In my own mind, as of September 2020, the school-to-prison pipeline runs through 1201 16th Street, NW and 555 New Jersey Avenue, NW, Washington DC!

Chapter 1

The Conventional Definition of the School-to-Prison Pipeline

D URING MY RUN for governor of the State of Connecticut in 2017 to 2018, the Connecticut Conference of the NAACP hosted a gubernatorial debate in April 2018 in New Haven concerning reentry prospects for former prisoners. Then candidate and now Governor Lamont attended as did then candidate Susan Byciewicz now lieutenant governor, Bridgeport mayor Joe Ganim, and businessman Guy Smith. The questions were asked of the candidates by ex-cons and was a decent exchange of ideas. I was the only Republican candidate there. A special guest in the audience was Reverend Tommie Jackson, who had coined the phrase "Life, Love, Liberty" for the weekly sermons at Faith Tabernacle Missionary Baptist Church in Stamford, Connecticut. It was the positive message of Reverend Tommie Jackson and "Life, Love, Liberty" that motivated me to run for governor in May 2017 after attending a Realtor rally in our state's capital, Hartford. The leading Democrat and Republican legislators spoke, with the exception of the governor, and they said absolutely nothing to indicate they had any idea of how to dig Connecticut out of its financial hole with anemic post-Great Recession growth, if what happened in Connecticut could be called growth.

It was under the tutelage of Reverend Tommie Jackson and the subsequent interim pastor, Dr. Boise Kimber, at Faith Tabernacle, along with the biweekly guest ministers from Norwalk, Bridgeport, Hartford, Newark, Queens, Manhattan, and other environs, that formed the genesis for this and other books. After the debate with my Democrat colleagues, photos were taken, and we were able to speak with some of the community members and ex-cons. I was gratified that some attendees had positive things to say about my debate messages, such as that the state puts needless roadblocks in the way of people to make their living, the poster child case being to get a license to cut hair, a thousand hours of barber school. In other cases, getting licenses to ply a trade or start your own business requires hiring your own attorney and paying them to sort your way through the morass of government regulations. One gentleman also appreciated my stand against poisoning our young people's brains with recreational marijuana instead focusing on the gift of life in sobriety. We met a few times after the meeting in and around Bridgeport. One of the meetings was at a church in Bridgeport that also ran reentry programs for ex-cons, trying to keep them on a straight path to avoid recidivism or doing it again and ending up back in jail. The church had a doorman for access purposes, but both confided that the ex-cons did show greater respect at the church versus a typical municipal building, because a church deserves respect. Amen.

It was here that this gentleman and the administrator of the reentry programs, who had also been one of the panelists at the NAACP debate, introduced me to the concept of a school-to-prison pipeline. This concept of a school ultimately leading to prison runs diametrically opposed to the assumption that school is a great leveler. According to former Secretary of Education Arne Duncan, Horace Mann, in the nineteenth century, called education "the great equalizer of the condition of men."[4]

But Secretary Duncan warned:

---

[4]   Quoted in "Education: the 'Great Equalizer,'" britannica.com.

> Students who receive a poor education, or who
> drop out of school before graduating, can end up
> on the wrong side of a lifelong gap in employ-
> ment, earnings, even life expectancy.[5]

When pressed, this gentleman and the administrator for the reentry program confirmed that there was not an actual plan in Hartford, the state's capital, of channeling students through school to prison to keep the state fully occupied as that would be too cynical. But let's look at what commonality public school and prison have.

The state runs both the public schools and the prisons. When we speak of the school-to-prison pipeline, we are not talking about expensive private schools like Brunswick for boys or Greenwich Academy for girls in Greenwich, or the namesake school for Horace Mann in the Riverdale section of the Bronx, where my very smart friend from New Rochelle went to high school. We are not speaking of the Ethical Culture Fieldston School in Riverdale either. We are definitely not speaking of the many catholic schools run by the Catholic church all across America. We are not speaking of boarding schools such as Phillips Academy in Andover, Massachusetts, where my good friend from Duke Law School attended, nor the plethora of private and religious schools all across our great land. And we are not even speaking about new and expanding public charter schools in their different iterations. No, we are talking about public schools located in communities where there are tough socioeconomic conditions, family breakdown, crime, and other challenges. These schools are primarily run by the state and are not public charter schools.

It should not come as a surprise that public unions are the dominant force at both public schools and at state prisons. This pipeline inquiry is more about who feeds the pipeline to keep a steady supply going as opposed to who receives our young citizens in jail. The prisons do the best they can with the limited resources that they are given in pay and physical plant. The prisons do not control the pipeline; they just receive misdemeanors and felons coming out of the pipe-

---

[5] Id.

line. And the pipeline is not about the many teachers who give of themselves every day to try to make a difference in the lives of young people who need the teachers' guidance and learning. Teaching is a high calling.

No, the pipeline is operated by the public unions and statists, in my opinion. Let's consider what a union is legally obligated to do. There is something that you may have come across in your own work, but it is definitely something that we learned in law school: fiduciary duty. "When someone has a fiduciary duty to someone else, the person with the duty must act in a way that will benefit someone else, usually financially."[6]

And a union owes its first fiduciary duty to its members. That would be the teachers. The second person the teachers' union owes a fiduciary duty to is itself. Children come into view third after the adults and the union. So by law, children are legally third in line for the duties owed by public unions. The mission statement of the National Education Association, the largest teachers' union, states, "We...are the voice of education professionals. Our mission is to advocate for education professionals." Why would the citizenry allow entities that put children third to monopolize our public school system? That is a breach of the public trust. And how do the public unions monopolize our schools? In the State of Connecticut in 2017, we had approximately nine thousand students in public charter schools K-12, which is a little less than about 2 percent of our public school population. The public unions have fought adamantly against increasing that number, and they have been successful. In 2017, according to the Connecticut State Department of Education, there were over 7,200 mostly black and Hispanic students on waitlists to get into a charter school.[7] That was an increase from the 6,762 students that were on a waitlist for the 2016–2017 school year.[8] More than 85 percent of students in public charter schools in Connecticut are either black

---

[6]   *Fiduciary Duty*, law.cornell.edu.
[7]   *Connecticut Charter Schools: Best Practices Annual Report 2017–2018*, p. 6.
[8]   Id.

or Hispanic with over 70 percent reported as low income in 2016.[9] But the state unions and statists[10] figuratively stand in the doors to charter schools to prevent more students from attending if they can help it. They will not allow the number of charter schools to increase.

The late Democrat Governor George Wallace would be so proud of the NEA and the AFT for standing in the door of charter schools and refusing to let black and Hispanic students into new or existing schools, lest the public unions' monopoly over public education be reduced just a little. This is just as Governor George Wallace did in 1963 when he led a "'stand-in-the-school-house-door' protest to prevent two black students from enrolling at the University of Alabama."[11] Governor Andrew Cuomo in New York used to be an unapologetic supporter of public charter schools in New York State. When demonstrations in favor of public charter schools would happen in Albany, large demonstrations of mostly "people of color," to use the current nomenclature, would plead with Albany to expand public charter schools to give greater educational choice to their children. Governor Cuomo would have positive things to say about those parents and charter schools. Now with Democrats moving significantly to the left, Governor Cuomo's championing of these underrepresented communities of color has faltered in the face of the march of the intolerants who oppose greater educational choice for high-needs students from communities of color. Allegations of sexual misconduct against Governor Cuomo in 2021 made it even less likely that he would stand up to the public school monopoly or the NEA and AFT on behalf of school choice for high-needs students.

---

[9] "Quick Facts: Public Charter Schools in Connecticut/2016," ConnCan, www.conncan.org.

[10] A statist favors the state over the citizen. A statist will increase the size and power of the state over the citizen, if given a chance.

[11] Quoted in biography.com.

Chapter 2

Advantages of Public Charter Schools

I DEALLY, IT SHOULD be enough that the parents and guardians desire for their children to attend a public charter school. Nobody knows their children better than the parents and guardians. Who is the state to question the choice of the parents and guardians? The state cannot know their children better than the parents and guardians. And our assumption is that parents and guardians have the best interests of their children at heart, particularly when you have to take extra measures to get into a public charter school. For a traditional public school, you merely move into the neighborhood and ask where the local elementary school, middle school, or high school is. Then you show your proof of residence, and then your child is in the school. To get into a public charter school, you actually have to find it as it may not necessarily be in your immediate vicinity, and then you have to fill out forms beyond what is necessary to get into your neighborhood school. This extra effort in and of itself would indicate that the parents and guardians of these children are looking out for them and trying to do what they believe is best for them. If the parents and guardians thought that the public charter school was not good for their children, for whatever reason, which could go beyond academics to class size or physical buildings or convenience for drop-off and pickup, that should be good enough for the state. It appears, however, that public charter schools have to prove that they are not just as good as conventional public schools, that they are in fact better. And if they are not better, then they may not merit consideration to remain open. Instead, the statists would push to close a public charter school that is merely as good as the local neighborhood school so as to bring the jobs and money that these students represent back into the local school system. But that is wrong as the parents and guardians of the children in the public charter school have judged it a better fit for their children. This is to whom we must be responsive and not the NEA or AFT and their surrogates. The children come first.

As public charter schools mature and get a longer track record, there is more data available on public charter schools generally and individual schools specifically. What if it turns out that students from public charter schools end up not only going to college at a higher rate but actually finishing two-year and four-year degrees at a higher rate than students from conventional public schools? That would be a positive. A legitimate countervailing consideration in favor of the data on conventional public schools is that conventional public schools have to take all comers. And not all students have parents or guardians who pay attention to their children's education for one year or many years. It can be granted that the input and positive reinforcement by parents and guardians to their children will empirically help their children's math, English, science, and other course performance. The public charter performance phenomenon is not an accident, however. There are some charters that don't make it, and their test numbers during their limited number of charter years were not good enough to receive an extension on their charter, so they were terminated or gave up their charter. And that is how the system is designed to work. That is why it is a "charter" school. It only gets limited lifespans from the state department of education, perhaps three, four, or five years. That allows the public to check in to see that some defensible education results are being achieved for the public dollar.

By the same token, however, a local public school has an indefinite shelf life. Unless the community goes out of business and everybody leaves, there will always be a local public school. That is as it should be. But there is a downside to that arrangement. What incentive does the local public school have to get better? It will still be open ten years from now. What incentive is there to eliminate ineffective teachers? We tend to like those that we work with. We identify with their lives and the lives of their families. To fire a person is an abrupt change in that person's life that few people want to do. Perhaps that person can be repurposed within the local school system. Perhaps they can be recycled. That is all human and understandable, but it can impede improvement of the education being delivered to the students at the school. If a public charter school doesn't make its numbers by the end of its limited charter, not only do the teachers risk being fired, but the entire administration risks being fired because the school would go out of business. The goal here is where it should be on the education of our children. For that reason, the limited charter of public charter schools can be an incentive to have better teacher accountability through educational results. In a local public school, there is a personal consideration to not fire an ineffective teacher but rather to recycle that teacher within the school system since the school will not go out of business and there may be significant public union collective bargaining protections for an employee of the school that makes it hard to fire ineffective teachers.

At the end of the day, if a public charter school is holding even or exceeding the results of the local school district, it would seem that the public charter would be entitled to an extension of their charter for another five years.

Chapter 3

Noteworthy Results of Stamford Charter School for Excellence

T HERE ARE COUNTLESS success stories of charter schools nationwide that teach majority, minority student bodies with high percentage of students from economic high-needs communities across the nation. This is not to slight any of their stellar performances, but a recently chartered school in my town has already done well, and it was not even five years old. Stamford Charter School for Excellence in Stamford, Connecticut, is doing more than yeoman's work in teaching their students. For the 2018–2019 school year, SCSE had expanded to 320 students. Fifty percent of their students were black, and 22 percent were Hispanic.[12] Half the children had reduced-price lunches, and almost 11 percent had limited English proficiency.[13] The data for grades three and four are positive and encouraging. These are students who had spent two or three years with the school. It would only add a new grade as their students graduated from one grade and moved to the next.

---

[12] Appendix A: 2018–19 Charter School Annual Report, Stamford Charter School for Excellence, Connecticut State Department of Education, October 18, 2019, p.18.

[13] Id.

Table A-2 of the SCSE annual report to the Connecticut State Department of Education showed their fourth graders achieving grade level scores or better in English language arts at 83.6 percent compared to 46.9 percent for Stamford Public Schools and 54.6 percent for all Connecticut public schools. That is thirty points above the entire state average, which would have lower high-needs students on average. Third graders at SCSE achieved grade level scores or better at 87.8 percent in English language arts, compared to 48.9 percent for Stamford public school third graders and 54.3 percent for all of Connecticut public school third graders.[14] Again, this exceeds the state average by thirty-four points. For the 50 percent of the student body at SCSE that was black, their English language arts score was at grade level or better at 83.3 percent compared to 31.3 percent for the Stamford School District and 33.2 percent for black third and fourth graders in Connecticut state public schools. That is fifty points above the state average. The math results at SCSE for black students scoring at or above their grade level were 91.7 percent compared to 20.5 percent for the Stamford public schools and 21.7 percent for black third and fourth graders in Connecticut state public schools.[15] That is seventy points above the state average! How long will the statists deny the efficacy of SCSE?

For the Hispanic students at SCSE, third and fourth graders' English language arts scores were at grade level or above at 73.3 percent compared to 35.3 percent in the Stamford School District and 34.1 percent for statewide Connecticut state public schools. That would be almost forty points better than the state average. The math scores had a similar achievement gap between the SCSE and the Stamford public schools and the statewide averages. The Hispanic students scored at grade level or above at 100 percent at SCSE versus 28.9 percent for the Stamford School District and 25.3 percent for statewide Connecticut public schools.[16] Seventy-five points above the statewide average is noteworthy. These are for students at a school where 60 percent of the

---

[14] Id., p. 8.
[15] Id.
[16] Id.

students come from families or homes with high needs.[17] If you were a parent or guardian of a black or Hispanic child, wouldn't you look twice at those results and consider whether there might be a different and better way for your children than the local public school, only to learn that public charter schools in Connecticut have been restricted by the statists so that there are almost as many black and Hispanic students on the waitlists to get in as there are attending public charter schools in Connecticut? Doesn't that amount to a scandal? These self-same statists hold themselves out as the proponents of the powerless, but they stand in the schoolhouse door and prevent the expansion and increased funding of these public charter schools!

These test results for the 2018–2019 school year at SCSE were the equivalent of an indictment not just of the Stamford public school system but the Connecticut public schools as well for what could be, but for the public school monopoly enforced by the NEA, AFT, and their statist allies. Does America not question when blacks and Hispanics get lower scores in math and English language arts than the average? We should not shrug our shoulders and accept the status quo under the public school monopoly that puts our children third in line behind the teachers and the public unions. More public charter schools and vouchers for private schools should be made available to high-needs students to unleash their proven potential.

The *Stamford Advocate*, owned by Hearst Publications, has, in my opinion, had a bias against the success of SCSE. From their reporting or lack thereof, it appears that they are opposed to the expansion of public charter schools as it is a potential diminution of the power of the state over the citizen. In my opinion, the *Stamford Advocate* does not like public charter schools as the paper cannot abide the decentralization of power. To take power away from the government interferes with ruling the citizenry by our betters. If the *Stamford Advocate* were asked about the performance of the SCSE after its filing of the 2018–2019 Charter School Annual Report with the Connecticut State Department of Education, what would they

---

[17] "How does Stamford Charter School for Excellence do it?" David Lucey, November 2, 2019, p. 5.

say? We don't know. My Internet search did not show any articles in the *Stamford Advocate* to laud one of the best performances of any public school in the state. That is cancel culture. If you don't write about it, it didn't happen. If you don't write about it, then nobody will know about success, where the paper rather not see success. Hearst has been a pioneer in cancel cancer, which is another name for cancel culture, as cancel cancer is dead on the inside. "Culture" indicates something living. "Cancel cancer," on the other hand, tries to kill what it tries to block from public discourse. There is nothing positive about cancel cancer. It is illiberal and dishonest. Where ideas should be discussed and tested through argument and debate, cancel cancer does not condone debate nor the exchange of ideas. If the *Stamford Advocate* did in fact write an article extolling the performance and results of SCSE, then I apologize for not finding it.

There is one political orthodoxy, and that is what will be sold. Some newspaper businesses, such as Hearst, have given up the objective reporting of events and happenings in society and replaced reporting with an ideologically based narrative based on their own informational bubble. The editors at Hearst Newspapers would have done well to move into the proposed community advertised in *Saturday Night Live*'s spoof commercial for a community in Brooklyn, "where everybody thinks the same."

"Wouldn't it be great to live in a place where everybody thinks like you?" This well-edited commercial went through the benefits of being in a bubble where everybody thinks like you and dresses like you. The punch line at the end is that "studios start at $600,000," which clearly indicates that this bubble community is meant only for the well-to-do who can't be bothered with those who don't think like them.

One of Hearst's sister publications, *Greenwich Time*, was my hometown newspaper for decades. Not only did I read it, but I placed ads in it to paint houses, draft wills, and sell used boats or cars. For many years, I would send letters to the editor, and sometimes they would publish them. An unfortunate thing happened to the *Greenwich Time* in 2008 as it and four other daily newspapers were acquired by Hearst Media.[18] The *Greenwich Time* serves the Town of Greenwich, which has been a Republican town for decades. In light of that reality, the editorial board of the *Greenwich Time* has had to hide its statist tendencies for fear of offending subscribers and advertisers but still run a business.

When I ran for governor of the State of Connecticut in 2017 to 2018, the concept of cancel cancer had not dawned on me. I was wholly inexperienced and unprepared for what I was undertaking, running for governor, but the message of "Life, Love, Liberty" from Faith Tabernacle Missionary Baptist Church in Stamford, Connecticut, was so strong that I believed it merited being driven around the State of Connecticut and expounded as "Gratitude, Common Humanity, and Liberty!" Faith Tabernacle is an African American Baptist church founded in 1947 and is in the heart of Stamford. I had been going there for a few years, and the message was so positive and motivational that the message needed to be shared beyond Faith. As an immigrant to America from West Germany, I am so grateful to our great land for the opportunities afforded people who immigrate here as well as efforts made by the United States to help other nations. My campaign was an effort to spread the positive messages that I had learned at Faith. I busily set about preparing my campaign platform and articles on the economy, state finances, immigration, prison reform, liberalization of our economy, pension deficits, and the like. Our new interim pastor was so kind as to help vet my platforms and positions. He mentored me through weekly meetings during my campaign. As I was often on the road traveling to Republican Town Committee meetings or working on more articles, such as a pitch to Amazon to select Stamford for its second headquarters, I did not notice that the *Greenwich Time* never called me to do a story on me, even though they knew I was running and lived in town. I did notice that they never published any of the letters to the editors or opinion pieces that I e-mailed them, but that was their political bias. Isn't a story about a local resident running for governor a story that can be written devoid of politics? But there was

---

[18] "Greenwich Time," wikipedia.com, accessed September 25, 2020.

not enough time during the campaign to focus on Greenwich, which was on the periphery of Connecticut.

In retrospect, a story on a resident of the Town of Greenwich who was running for governor seems like a natural thing to do for the *Greenwich Time*! I was not a recent transplant. We had moved to Greenwich in 1963. I had gone to the Greenwich public school system from K-12 and was a member of the class of 1978. I had gone to First Congregational Church from the 1960s all the way through to around 2016. I had even been a Sunday school teacher there for seven years. My time at First Congregational would have been close to or exceeding fifty years with time out for when I went off to Vermont for college or Ohio and North Carolina for law school. Time was also spent living in New York City as a young lawyer. Nonetheless, I established my law practice in Old Greenwich in 1989. I got married in Greenwich in 1994. All three of my daughters were born at Greenwich Hospital. All three of my daughters were baptized and confirmed at First Congregational Church and attended Greenwich public schools from K-12 and all graduated from Greenwich High School. I have run my building business, Harbor Builders, in Greenwich since 1995, during which time I renovated or built about twenty new homes. It would seem that such a candidate with such local roots might merit an article in the *Greenwich Time* during the campaign. But that did not happen as the *Greenwich Time* is and was a pioneer of cancel cancer. During the same electoral cycle of 2017–2018, a Democrat woman in town declared to run for a statewide post either in the Democratic Party or for a Democrat slot, and that merited a front-page story, above the fold. The writer was able to squeeze the word *progressive* into the article about this Democrat candidate from Greenwich at least eight times. How exciting.

If you are not running a program endorsed by statists, the chances that you get a fair hearing from Hearst Media is slight. Hindsight is twenty-twenty, and we see the stellar results of SCSE for 2018–2019 as one of the best schools in the state, but the reporting by the *Stamford Advocate*, a Hearst Media publication, panned the school in May 2017. The school had only been founded in 2015 and was an offshoot from an acclaimed public charter school in the Bronx,

New York. The title of the hit piece tells much of the gist of the story: "Stamford charter school faces challenges, mixed reviews."[19] It is a "hit" piece not because it harkens to a top 40 hit song but because it is more like a mafioso doing a hit on a rival gangster and killing the rival gangster. That is the depth to which the *Advocate* stooped. After opening with a story of a mother who withdrew here two boys from SCSE and whose boys now missed the SCSE, the author commences with the parade of horribles: "financial challenges" and "criticism for what some say is a failure to provide resources for special-needs students." This is for a new school that at the time had all of 164 students. "[S]chool lacks occupational and physical therapists a speech pathologist and a psychologist or behavioral analyst." Newspapers are always able to get allies of the state to criticize public charter schools. Here they used a "local parent advocate" and a former state legislator to criticize the SCSE for "failing to appropriately serve special-needs students and non-native English speakers." And then the death-knell:

"Charter schools are an increasingly controversial topic across the country, with supporters—the biggest among them being *Donald Trump's* education secretary *Betsy DeVos*—defending them as much-needed choice for less-traditional learners and critics calling them a threat to quality public education. (emphasis in original)" The paper slandered SCSE before it even opened in 2014: "public school parents circulated a petition against the school and the city's *Board of Education* held a symbolic vote opposing the plan." The public teachers' unions can always find allies in the local PTA and other parents to oppose school choice. Who wants to disagree with their local teachers, whom we all love and respect? They rightfully stand on a pedestal.

The hit piece by the *Stamford Advocate* continued that the SCSE "was not able to hire a guidance counselor, specialty teachers and other positions that year 'due to budgetary restraints.'" That all sounds rational, given that they only had 164 students. Ultimately, the author panned the SCSE with "mixed" reviews. The closer was that Jonathan Pelto, a former state legislator, said that SCSE was "a

---

[19] Nelson Oliverra, *Stamford Advocate*, May 6, 2017.

prime example" of how charters "fail to provide" an appropriate education to minority children. This is an odd conclusion to a hit piece that contained the fact in it that at that time, two-thirds of the 164 SCSE students were black, and about one quarter were Hispanic. The story acknowledged that SCSE reported that it typically appeals to families and populations in high-needs communities that have been traditionally underserved. Remarkable that pioneers in cancel cancer would even allow that heresy to be published. But that in a nutshell is what school choice is about. What of a study by the Center for Research on Education Outcomes at Stanford University in California that "found that [public] charter schools do a better job teaching low income students, minority students and students who are still learning English than traditional schools."[20] Where is the piece by the *Stamford Advocate* touting loud and clear the stellar test results of SCSE? If a tree falls in the forest and nobody is around to hear it, does it make a noise? That is the tactic of cancel cancer—trying to defeat school choice for students of color by deafening silence.

It is not a stretch to say that black and Hispanic students have not been in school districts with A-1 resources. To present these black and Hispanic students in economically challenged communities with different educational alternatives is a social good. Anything that threatens the width and breadth of state institutions or to lessen the number of public union jobs, the statists cry foul and try to oppose whatever threatens the state. Cue the *Advocate's* hit piece.

In light of the subsequent stellar results at SCSE for the 2018–2019 academic year, that would merit a follow-up story by the *Stamford Advocate* that all their talk about mixed results was misplaced. No school will be perfect. But when the students are exceeding the test results of Stamford public schools and public schools statewide by far, that calls for compliments and adoption of similar strategies. But the *Stamford Advocate* has not boldly admitted its error against SCSE. More cancel cancer.

---

[20] "Public Charter School Students Graduate from College at Three to Five Times National Average," *National Alliance for Public Charter Schools*, press release, July 27, 2017.

When blogger David Lucey took the time to look at the testing data and compare it to other schools, it was clear that SCSE was delivering for its students. He took the top fifty schools in Connecticut by test results and put the English and math results of those schools and the SCSE results in one graph. SCSE was right there with these top 10 percent schools from the rest of Connecticut, which "are mostly from affluent towns with high per pupil spending and likely have a high percentage of stay-at-home parents. They also generally have lower percentages of high-needs students…[compared to SCSE] with over 60% having high needs."[21] That is newsworthy, but not to the opponents of school choice. Mr. Lucey made the further observation:

> Since SCSE costs less than half the state-wide average per pupil, and one quarter of the costliest school districts…[if Stamford] could operate all of its schools at a similar cost, it would reduce spending by about $190,000,000…out of annual budgeted expenses of about $505,000,000… This leaves aside the much higher pension costs attributed to town school districts than to charters picked up by the state.[22]

That analysis is overly generous as the City of Stamford offers team sports and various student activities that a charter may not, as well as caring for special-needs students. But nonetheless, financial savings could be realized if the public charter school model were more broadly embraced. It is the loss of union dues and the generally lower pay for charter school teachers and administrators that alarms the AFT and NEA, as well as the statists who fight against reductions in the size and scope of the state vis-à-vis the citizenry.

---

[21] "How does Stamford Charter School for Excellence do it?" November 2, 2019, accessed September 24, 2020.

[22] Id., p. 5–7.

Chapter 4

Public Charter School Students Graduate College at a Higher Rate Than Those from the Public School Monopoly

C OLLEGE IS NOT for everyone, and not everyone was meant for college. The average plumber makes as much as the average attorney. The plumber did not have to go to four years of undergraduate college and then three years of law school to get a law degree. That all required time and tuition. A plumber could be an apprentice with a plumber and take plumbing classes at night and still earn money the entire time. It is true that a person could take college and law school at night, but those seven years of full-time college and law school are not going to happen in seven long years! The vast majority of attorneys are sole practitioners, just as I was after working at a small law firm in Manhattan before starting my practice. In an information society, it is anticipated that college-trained people will be in higher demand than non-college trained. In addition, the College Board reported in *Education Pays 2016* that "college education is associated with healthier lifestyles, reducing health care costs." A Georgetown University report claimed that most of the 11.6 million new jobs that were created after the Great Recession went to workers with at least some college education, and 72 percent of those jobs went to workers with at least a bachelor's degree.[23] Naturally, one should not be surprised that an entity that calls itself the College Board would write that a college education is very important, but that is a safe assumption.

On the other side of the coin, however, is the risk of credential-ization, where the minimum job requirement that human resource departments put on jobs that they require some college or a four-year degree to be considered for a job may be excessive. A closer look at the people actually doing the work and what is required to do the work may reveal that a college degree is in fact not essential. When that happens, then it makes it harder for blacks, specifically, who have one tenth of the net worth of white Americans, to compete for those jobs as there is a lower percentage of college graduates in the black community. And going to college requires resources.

A human resources department should not put down that a college degree is required unless that is absolutely the case. Nonetheless, it is relevant to see whether going to a conventional public school or going to a public charter school might change the college trajectory of a student. No surprise to some but a surprise to statists, going to public charter schools does actually change the trajectory of the student. Not only are some public charter schools far outperforming conventional public schools academically, they are doing so beyond graduation.

According to the 74 Million, a charter school advocate, "[o]nly about nine percent of children from the lowest-income families go on to complete college within six years. The charter school networks featured in *The Alumni* are graduating college at significantly higher rates."[24] For a public charter school network called Uncommon Schools, 50 percent of their graduates were finishing four-year colleges after six years. KIPP public charter schools had a 38 percent graduation rate. YES Prep Public Schools reported a 47 percent graduation rate. Achievement First showed a 32 percent graduation rate. Not all public charter schools are going to outstrip the average of

---

[23] Id., "Public Charter School Students Graduate from College at Three to Five Times National Average."

[24] Id.

conventional public schools, but these are impressive numbers. And it should go without saying that if 50 percent of your graduates are finishing four-year degrees in six years, then that leaves even fewer graduates for the school-to-prison pipeline. Can that even be a thing for the rest of the student body? To go to prison?

While it is legitimate to consider that public charter school students can do better academically because their parents and guardians had already taken the time to look outside of the conventional neighborhood school as an alternative choice for their children, that these same parents and guardians might take more time to help their children achieve, it is also legitimate to consider that the parents and guardians have to attend parent-teacher conferences and to receive communications from their children's school. In those communications with parents and guardians, there may be repeated reminders of what comes after K-12. What are the plans thereafter? What are the goals for the child? What is the plan? A truism spoken by Dr. Boise Kimber at Faith Tabernacle was this: "If you don't have a plan, then you have a plan to fail!" Consider that? If you go from day to day and week to week and you are merely punching the clock in your life without really thinking where you would like to be in two or five years or what you would like to accomplish, then in two or five years, you will be in the same place. You have the gift of life. Every day is a gift. If you don't take advantage of that gift by designing a plan for yourself, then that gift is being squandered. How are you going to improve yourself or make the life of your children, family, friends, and/or community better? The focus of a conventional public school, public charter school, and private school is to educate the student so that he or she may be able to be a better productive citizen and one who can participate in our democracy. The public charter school focuses on test results, for better or worse, as are conventional public schools, but public charter schools are also looking at what the child will be doing after graduation. These high graduation rates from four-year college programs is a strong indicator considering that the majority of students in these public charter schools are from high-needs families. And at all events, the goal is to avoid the school-to-prison pipeline run by the AFT and NEA.

"For high-income whites or Asian parent, these degree-earning rates will not impress. Among those parents, *79 percent* of their children earn four-year degrees within six years after graduating from high school."[25] "But because charter networks almost exclusively educate low-income and minority students, the question has to be framed differently. The challenges faced by these students are incomparable to children from most upper-income families."[26]

One should not lose sight of the fact that public charters are a recent phenomenon of the past few decades. They have not been with us for fifty years. Minnesota was the first state to pass laws enabling the creation of charter schools in 1991.[27] California followed the next year in 1992. By 2015, forty-three states and the District of Columbia had charter school legislation.[28] It is too early to judge many charter schools on the metric of their students enrolling and graduating from four-year colleges in six years, but the signs from those public charters that have been in existence long enough are encouraging. "If these rising success rates prove to be true, the civil rights and anti-poverty implications are significant."[29]

Has there been an anti-poverty program or War on Poverty program that could ever boast such results for children from high-needs families? Which one? And the opponents of public charter schools champion themselves as advocates for the poor? It would seem more accurate that the opponents of public charter schools are champions of adults before children.

Not to be lost in this discussion is a phenomenon that the public charter schools like KIPP found was that their graduates had a higher probability of getting an undergraduate degree, the higher ranked that college or university was.

---

[25] "The Alumni," Richard Whitmire, July 26, 2017.

[26] Id.

[27] "Charter Schools in the United States," *History*, en.m.wikipedia.org, accessed September 29, 2020.

[28] Id.

[29] Whitmore, "The Alumni."

In some cases, that range can be dramatic: 90-plus percent success at an elite college, compared with 15 percent or even lower at non-selective universities.[30]

It is not surprising that highly selective colleges and universities may have better endowments and the financial wherewithal to assist high-needs students to see them through four years of college. For that reason, some public charters have made the effort in their college counseling to get their students to universities and colleges that have a better success rate at graduating their students. In other words, the public charter school does not see its job as done when their students graduate from twelfth grade. Imagine that some public charter schools are now calling their classes not the year that they graduate from high school but rather the projected graduation year from a four-year college four years hence. Thus the class of 2026 from high school would be the class of 2030. These are experiments worth trying. Incubators of success. "Many small but selective colleges that have traditionally enrolled nearly all-white student bodies, and are located in rural communities in states such as Pennsylvania and Ohio are proving to be great collaborators with inner-city charters."[31]

Not that that is necessarily a panacea as it can be a cultural transition to go from a high-needs background to a rural campus with students primarily from middle-class and upper-class backgrounds.

Compare that to the Head Start childhood education program that was originally started in 1965 to help as a summer school program for low-income children to learn before the actual beginning of school. It has since ballooned to include early childhood education, health, nutrition, and parent-involved services for low-income children and families.[32] While the Head Start program certainly helps, is society getting as much out of it as it costs? Could these dollars be used more effectively to help low-income children and their families? The Welfare-Industrial Complex does not necessarily want to ask that question as that may require changing part of the Welfare-Industrial

[30] Id.
[31] Id.
[32] "Head Start (program)," en.m.wikipedia.org, accessed September 29, 2020.

Complex. There are too many jobs, salaries, health care benefits, pension benefits, sick days, personal days, and disability benefits tied up in the Welfare-Industrial Complex to make any significant changes without a swift and forceful reaction by such Complex to defend its turf and the jobs and positions of its staff. Thus we plod along and are prohibited from asking: Is there a better way?

Public charter schools are definitely a different way. They are incubators for change and different approaches. Not all will be successful. And some will be more successful than others. So then you adopt the model that is more effective, but you do not prevent further experimentation and new ideas to learn what gets even better results. For the cancel cancer crowd of statists, they do not want to learn of public charter school successes as it may mean that conventional public schools, the backbone of our nation's school system, may have to change and adapt to compete with new ideas and methods coming from public charter schools. The easier response is reaction and obstruction of change and the suppression of public charter schools. That is the simple power politics at play.

Chapter 5

The Positive Impact of Colocating Public Charter Schools in the Same Building as a Neighborhood School

FOR THE AFT, NEA, and their statists allies inside and outside of government who wish to limit and squash opportunities for students of color to excel in the public charter school environment, reading names such as KIPP Public Charter Schools or Achievement First pains them as these opponents wish these institutions and series of schools had never been invented. Professor Sarah Cordes at Temple University did an extensive study of the impact of public charter schools on traditional public schools not just colocated in the same building but also the impact of being half a mile or further away. The data analyzed went from 1996 to 2010. "Exposure to charter schools significantly increased student performance at nearby traditional public schools."[33]

Traditional public schools that share space with another traditional public school saw no increase in academic performance. Only if the traditional public school shared space with a public charter

---

[33] "Charter schools have positive effects on traditional public schools located near them, at least in New York City," Jamie Davies O'Leary, fordhaminstitute.org, August 18, 2017.

school did the traditional public school see an academic improvement in its students.

A novel proposition is that public charter schools be co-located in all traditional public schools. The facilities are there. The after-school sports programs would still be available to all the students in the school as well as after-school programs that did not involve sports. The parents and guardians of the students could decide whether they wanted their children in the traditional public school part of the school or in the public charter part. Perhaps the student body representation would shift between the two sides as the fortunes of one or the other rose faster than the other? The obvious beneficiaries would be the children.

This is the problem for the opponents of public charter schools. Putting public charter schools in the same buildings as conventional public schools brings comparisons and competition that the opponents of public charter schools would rather not broach. If a public charter school can achieve higher results with mostly minority and high-needs student bodies, then traditional public schools will be pressured to follow similar teaching methods. That is good for the students and the traditional public schools. As public charter schools are less likely to be unionized, each of these schools represents a missed opportunity for the NEA and AFT to have more public union members and union dues to support the statist endeavor of more state. It is sad, but the opponents of public charter schools are not proponents of the students of color at these institutions. Instead of cheering for the educational steps taken, the opponents wish for the demise of these public charters and draft intricate requirements and standards at the state level in the hope of using those intricate requirements and standards to prevent more public charters from being created and to take away the charters of existing public charter schools. It is so cynical. Adults against children. It's not a fair competition.

Chapter 6

Private Schools Tend to Encourage the Success Sequence to the Consternation of Statists

THIS BOOK ADDRESSES the true school-to-prison pipeline aided and abetted by the structural statism of the statists that puts the interest of the state above the interests of the citizens. The school-to-prison pipeline is not about what happens when administrators put safety officers in schools to try to make it a more secure learning environment for all students. The school-to-prison pipeline is about funneling as many kids through the public school monopoly to the exclusion of school choice for our children from high-needs communities.

The facilitators of the school-to-prison pipeline also stumble at the mention of the *success sequence*. The success sequence is a straightforward approach to people achieving greater economic, mental, and physical health in their lives. It basically says that a person should graduate from high school and/or college, if possible, get a job, get married, and only then have children. Critics are apoplectic at this core recommendation as they are convinced that no matter how hard somebody tries, they will never make it because of inherent injustices in our country. Some of the critics of the success sequence are adherents of determinism: (1) the doctrine that everything is entirely determined by a sequence of causes and (2) the doctrine that one's choice of action is not free but is determined by a sequence of causes independent of his will.[34] These determinists selectively ignore the fact that if an individual is married and regularly attends a mosque, church, synagogue, or temple, there is only a 10 percent chance that person will be dependent on the state for his or her bread, regardless of what the person's socioeconomic background was.

The critics of the success sequence are likely one and the same as the opponents of school choice for our black, Hispanic, white, Asian, and other children from high-needs communities. It is their support of structural statism that reinforces obstacles to advancement for our brothers and sisters from high-needs communities. Author Brian Alexander, no relation, penned a piece in the *Atlantic*, a properly conformist publication in support of the power of the state: "What is the 'Success Sequence' and Why Do so Many Conservatives Like it?" The title already tips the hand that if a conservative likes it, then it is probably bad. He then opens with a strawman, which are always easy to swat down: "[A] coterie of pundits and think-tank scholars have arrived at a *surefire answer*, a simple one that comes with a snappy title and puts the onus on the individual to pursue the "success sequence.""[35]

Generally, anyone who suggests that they have a surefire answer is probably wrong. So author Alexander has already won the argument in the first paragraph. Well done. Just as public charter schools and vouchers are not a surefire answer to the woes that confront our children from high-needs communities, the success sequence is not a guarantor of success either. But what was it in life that was guaranteed? Death and taxes. That is about it. Not satisfied, Alexander steps in it by observing that the "success sequence, trustworthy as it may sound, conveniently frames *structural inequalities* as matters of individual choice."[36] He steps in it

---

[34] *Webster's New World Dictionary of the American Language*, College ed., The World Publishing Company, Cleveland, 1964.

[35] "What is the 'Success Sequence' and Why Do So Many Conservatives Like It?" atlantic.com, July 31, 2018.

[36] Id., emphasis added.

because he might have been referring in part to what some called structural racism in the protests and riots following the killing of African American George Floyd in May 2020, which in fact is by and large almost identical to structural statism. Structural statism is the hurdles, burdens and barriers placed in the way of the poor to earn their keep, to put a roof over their head, to put food on the plate of their children, and to pursue their happiness as they see fit by the state and its proponents. And part of structural statism is the subject of this book—how the statists use their political muscle and skills to deny school choice for children from high-needs communities. Alexander was fair enough to mention testimony of Nicholas Zill to the United States House Subcommittee on Human Resources, where Mr. Zill "presented data showing that 45 percent of children in single-parent families lived in poverty, versus 8 percent of children in married-couple families."[37] Alexander continued with work by historian and writer Barbara Dafoe Whitehead that "[t]he marriage part for me has more to do with a secure environment for kids to grow up in families than it is advice for young people to get married." And that is precisely the point. One of our primary concerns in government is the raising of children. Generally speaking, children are defenseless, whereas a single adult needs far less assistance to survive. This is why the state can remove a child from an unsafe environment. The standard for an adult would be mental incompetence.

To let you know where Alexander is coming from, he throws in the "fact" of "the role of late-20th century American-style capitalism in pushing families into financial insecurity." Yet the whole point of the success sequence is that if you hold to marriage, then you are less likely to realize financial insecurity. Two is better than one in making ends meet. And two parents together increase the educational, physical, and emotional health of their children. Those are the two sides of the success sequence. He referred to historian Whitehead again: "Any promotion of personal responsibility and the success sequence...

---

[37] Id.

should take a back seat to addressing the growing institutional barriers that make it difficult to raise a family out of poverty."

Unwittingly, Whitehead and Alexander have again referred to structural statism by citing "institutional barriers." In their minds, all is lost when "so much of one's prospects are determined by birth... especially when paired with capitalism, democracy still creates winners and losers."[38] Perhaps they would counsel that only more power and resources to the state can alleviate this situation. That is the customary default. More of the same with the illogical hope for a different outcome. Instead, of more of the same, there should be an expansion of school choice.

The refrain that there is nothing we can do about our circumstances unless the state steps in and helps is a well-worn pitch. But that is a false narrative. All the immigrants who try to enter the United States legally and illegally are all trying to improve their personal condition through free will, whether they come from Mexico, Honduras, Nigeria, the Philippines, Kenya, China, Haiti, Poland, etc. They are not concerned about these deterministic elements that would prevent them from improving the lives of their children or their own lives. And what of the truth that without the proper morals and values, an individual cannot reach their potential? The morals and values that a person brings with them do influence their trajectory through life. It is the reluctance of the public school system and the statists to speak of morals and values outside of the scope of what qualifies for political correctness that hurts out children. Bourgeois values of punctuality, hard work, study, respect, cleanliness, thrift, honor, service, etc. are not irrelevant. At the end of his story on the success sequence in the *Atlantic*, Alexander is able to give the success sequence a proper burial that it is as an "empty platitude" [used] to justify "all sorts of inequities." There you have it. And you thought suggesting ways for success for your children and yourself might be a positive thing. It ends up as an empty platitude justifying all sorts of inequities. Disregard that school choice is directly aimed at address-

---

[38] Id.

ing all sorts of inequities and the success sequence seeks to elevate citizens and their children above these same inequities.

Public charter schools can do just that. A study of private schools, religious schools, and traditional public schools found that the children of these different schools had significantly different trajectories even after controlling for students' race/ethnicity, parental education, family background, and family finances.[39] A report by the Institute for Family Studies and the American Enterprise Institute looked at attendance at public, Catholic, Protestant, and secular private schools and how that impacted on outcomes later in life. It was a survey of adults and how they were doing in life. One might expect certain results by Catholic schools in morals and values to exceed those of general public schools, which they did, but more remarkable was how Protestant private schools did even better. Only 11 percent of Protestant school attendees said they had a child out of wedlock versus 25 percent for public school attendees. Only 42 percent of public school attendees had gotten married, 53 percent for secular private school attendees, and 63 percent for Protestant school attendees. The National Longitudinal Survey of Youth 1997 found that 83 percent of teens who attended a Protestant school said most kids in their grade had not used illegal drugs versus only about 25 percent of public school kids. Similar results were found for more sex for public school children and less sex for kids in Catholic and Protestant schools. "[A]dults raised in financially disadvantaged families were especially likely to form intact marriages if they'd gone to a Catholic or Protestant school."[40]

Why should this matter? Because this is about children. The school-to-prison pipeline is about children. School is not just about pluses and minuses. School is not just about reading lessons and grammar. There is also an ecology to the school. What is the value system that you are around? What are the expectations for conduct between students and to teachers? What is the expectation to do your work on time and to hand it in? What kind of a citizen do you aspire

[39] "Private schools outpace public schools in putting kids on the path to marriage," W. Bradford Wilcox, Patrick J. Wolff and Peyton Roth, NationalReview.com, September 22, 2020.
[40] Id.

to be? Does the school teach the value of life—that the life of a fellow student or of a teacher has value and is inviolate? Does the school teach the Golden Rule to do unto others as you would have done unto yourself? These basic lessons were absent from Victor Cruz who shot his fellow students at the Parkland School shooting in Florida in 2018. It is anticipated that there are more single-parent households in the public school system than in private schools, and to avoid making people uncomfortable, the issue of the success sequence may be avoided. But that is not doing a service to our children. They have a right to know. They have a right to hear it discussed and what the outcomes can be. Better jobs come with graduating. Better economics come with marriage and waiting to have children until after you get married. That cannot always be achieved, and it may not be realistic for everyone, but it tends to produce better results. At no point is the success sequence a surefire answer, nor has it been proposed as such. Rather, it is part of an entire ecology of values that may be present in a public charter school or a religious private school. It is for these benefits that parents and guardians wish their children to attend. Would it surprise you if a drug dealer wanted his or her children to go to a public charter school? It shouldn't. He or she wants what is best for his or her children, just as you do.

The success sequence is more than a bumper sticker. It can be part of an entire ecology that includes academics, morals, and values to help a student achieve his or her potential. Policy makers should not reflexively defend the state but instead should see how they can offer more school choice to children from economically challenged communities. How can the costs of private school be ameliorated by vouchers so that the advantages of private school and the family advantages of private school can be offered to poor children?

Chapter 7

Connecticut's Abysmally Low Number of Public Charter Schools

ONNECTICUT HAS LESS than 2 percent of all public school
students in public charter schools, which is unrealistic. The
state's black and Hispanic communities who could benefit
the most due to lower-performing public schools in their districts
are wholly underserved. This result is entirely intentional due to the
power of the statists and public teacher unions to prevent the expansion of public charter schools, lest the pubic teacher unions have
fewer dues-paying members, and town and city administrators have
to do more accounting work to keep the ledgers straight on public
charter schools and conventional public schools. That may not be
the case in your state. It would not be realistic to expect a public
charter to outscore the performance of the average Connecticut state
school by so much as SCSE has done or to expect a charter school to
outscore their local schools. That would be too high a hurdle to put
in front of public charter schools, and it would be unfair. What is not
unrealistic, however, is to allow students who want to try this alternative form of public school to be able to go. It should be enough
that the charter school scores around the state average and the district
average. The reason that should be enough to allow a public charter
school to exist is that respect must be given to the choice of the citi-

zen over the power machinations of the state. Under the Connecticut State Constitution, "all free governments are instituted for the benefit of the citizen."[41] This means that the will of the citizen should prevail over the power machinations of factions that seek to use government to further their own goals at the expense of the public and to the detriment of our children.

---

[41] Article 1, Section 2 of the Connecticut State Constitution.

Chapter 8

Two Types of Public
Education Alternatives:
Public Charters and Vouchers

T HERE ARE TWO public alternatives to traditional union-run primary and secondary schools: charter schools and vouchers. In Connecticut, charter schools are public schools but are run by private entities that receive a charter to run a public school for a set amount of years, say five years, before the state board of education reviews their performance again. If the charter satisfies the board of education at five years that they are meeting or exceeding their performance criteria, the state extends their charter for a new time frame. If the charter does not meet their performance standards, it might be put on probation or shut down. Charters in Connecticut received $11,250 per student from the state in 2019. Generally, it costs more than that to teach one student, so the charters must raise money from the private sector and from people like you and me to make up the difference. What enervates the public unions and makes them dead set against charters is that most charters are not unionized, although there are numerous unionized charter schools. About 21 percent of Connecticut's public charter schools were unionized in 2016–2017. This means that fewer union dues will be paid by the teachers to union bosses and sent on to headquarters like the National Education Association or the American Federation of Teachers, who then use that money and their great resources to push their statist agenda. A charter school represents a potential loss of students to the traditional public school system by shifting the students to a different type of public school and the loss of teaching slots in the neighborhood school and the loss of union dues to the union bosses.

Legally, the public union has to fight school choice for poor kids as the second fiduciary responsibility of the union is to itself before our children at position three. That means that a public union will not work to put itself out of business. Instead, the public union is constantly working to try to assure that it has life and is growing. As a result, the public unions work very hard against school choice. An example would be AFT Connecticut, "a statewide labor federation of more than 90 local unions throughout the state."[42] "AFT Connecticut is a proud affiliate of the 1.5 million-member American Federation of Teachers (AFT), The 10-million member American Federation of Labor-Congress of Industrial Organizations (AFL-CIO) and the 200,000 member Connecticut AFL-CIO."[43]

This union-affiliated organization continues and will give you "The Truth About Charter Schools." "[C]harter schools have failed to share their innovations with public schools. What's more charter schools have actually increased racial and ethnic isolation in Connecticut's student communities."

And it gets worse as they question which patriots dare to offer more school choice to our poorest. "The corporate takeover of public education is underway."[44]

They point out that some charter schools in Michigan are run by for-profit organizations. "This should be deeply, deeply troubling for anyone thinking about their child's future education, or the future of this country."[45]

Yes, and there were only about nine thousand authorized charter slots in Connecticut in 2017, and there were almost seven thousand mostly black, Hispanic, and Asian children on a waitlist to get

---

[42] *About Us,* August 1, 2019, aft.org.
[43] Id.
[44] Id., quoted Erik Kain.
[45] Quoting Erik Kain.

into a charter school as the statists have capped the number of seats to deny these children school choice. If your children lose as a result of the priorities of adults, then the AFT seems to say, "Tough luck for your children."

Chapter 9

Vouchers and School Choice

I N ADDITION, TO expand school choice for students from high-needs socioeconomic communities, let the state give vouchers to students that they can take to a non-religious or religious private school like a Catholic school. There are bigots who will say that the state should not give any money to a religious school. But this is cutting off our nose to spite our face. The religious schools give results in higher math, English, and postsecondary school studies. Supreme Court Justice Sonia Sotomayor is a hearty proponent of the Catholic school she attended as a young girl. She attended the Blessed Sacrament School in the Bronx from kindergarten through eighth grade, [46] which was close to the Bronxdale Houses public housing complex where she lived. According to writer Greg Kandra, for people who were members of the Blessed Sacrament parish, the annual tuition was $2,900. Justice Sotomayor continued with her education to receive her undergraduate degree at Princeton University and her law degree at Yale University. This is not the everyday person's trajectory. But vouchers can give poor students options that they would

---

[46] Greg Kandra writing in *Beliefnet,* "Roots: Visiting Sotomayor's Catholic grade school."

not otherwise have had, and it is cheaper than paying for that student in a regular public school. Vouchers do not typically cover a student's entire tuition at a religious school. Rather, they make it more afford-able. A religious or other private school might give a scholarship to a student. The student's family might contribute the balance of the tuition. Anything to get the young person a little better chance. So why oppose it? Why stop the pipeline?

How is it that we allow the public unions to control what happens in Connecticut when students are third in line after adults and the union? The NEA website boasts that "our mission is to advocate for education professionals." That is accurate. But how does that square with their statement on equal opportunity: "All students have the human and civil right to a quality public education."[47] The NEA, however, went further and boasted in a newspaper headline on its home page "Strikes, Pay Rises and Charter Protests: America's Exhausting Exhilarating Year."[48] So the NEA finds protesting against charters exhilarating? How sad. But the Realpolitik of the NEA is to promote the interest of adults before children. Yes, the pipeline runs right through the headquarters of the NEA at 1201 16th Street, NW, Washington, DC.

---

[47] NEA.org *mission statement.*
[48] NEA.org, July 27, 2019.

Chapter 10

A Missed Opportunity—*Sheff v O'Neill*

CAPPING THE NUMBER of charter schools and how many students of color can attend them is a victory for the public unions and their allied statists and a testament to their political muscle. To get an idea of how important it is to keep as many students in the union dues-paying environment, consider the decades-long litigation to challenge school funding in Connecticut: *Sheff v. O'Neill*, 238 Conn 1, 678 A.2d 1267 (1996). It began in 1989 by eighteen school-aged children in Hartford, the capital of Connecticut, challenging the funding of schools in Connecticut under the Connecticut Constitution in majority black and Latino school districts, where students had less resources spent on them than in mostly white districts. In 1996, the Connecticut Supreme Court ruled that the state had an affirmative obligation to provide Connecticut's schoolchildren with substantially equal educational opportunity.[49] More motions were made. Settlements were made. There were to be magnet and regional charter schools. But if you fast-forward to 2019, there are now greater types of public schools found in Hartford, but public charter schools were not significantly

---

[49] As reported in *Wikipedia, "Sheff v O'Neil."*

expanded! Why? Because the public unions control the state, and the children come third to the statists. For whatever the arguments made about the interest of the student, these same advocates won't release the students from the state system, the school-to-prison pipeline.

Are charters a panacea? Not precisely, but they should be given a chance. New Orleans has allowed 79 percent of their public schools to be public charter schools; Detroit has allowed 51 percent of their public schools to be public charter schools; 36 percent in Flint, Michigan; and 35 percent in Gary, Indiana.[50] These are majority black municipalities. They are at least trying public charter schools. They are at least offering their constituents more school choice. Would an opponent of public charter schools at least concede that these jurisdictions are trying to do what is right by their students to the best of the resources that they have at hand? If majority-minority jurisdictions will try public charter schools for their students, why must a state like Connecticut, which is not majority minority, refuse to try and at the same time keep public charter schools capped at 2 percent of the student population when it is primarily black and Hispanic students who would benefit most? It is the parents and guardians who know their children best. And these parents and guardians are trying to get them into a public charter school, but the statists are working hard to deny the parents and guardians of black and Hispanic students that choice. How is this enlightened? Did not many politicians and statists in Connecticut get on their soapboxes after the killing of George Floyd and Breonna Taylor in 2020 and say how they would fight structural racism? That they would try to increase the chances for African Americans? And yet these self-same statists work with the AFT and NEA to put roadblocks in the way of school choice for black and Hispanic students. Aren't the roadblocks and hurdles that the statists put in the way of black and Hispanic students to get ahead, structural racism?

---

[50]   As reported by Lyndsey Leyton, *The Washington Post,* "New Orleans leads nation in percentage of public charter school enrollment," December 10, 2013.

Chapter 11

Students Should have Greater Choices and the Parkland School Shooting

L ET THE PARENTS, guardians, and students decide, not the statists. Research is finding not just better mathematics and English results for charters.[51] The follow-up after high school has been better with attendance and actual graduation rates from four-year institutions. It is higher for charter schools than public schools.[52] That is a desirable outcome.

The statists counter that the charter's cherry-pick the best students because they have motivated parents and guardians and leave the not-best students in the public schools, which makes it an uphill battle to achieve results for traditional public schools. It is not fair to students to be held back because of others. It is not fair to make students be in schools where there is lower perceived physical safety. Consider the debacle of the Parkland shooting in Florida in 2018. The Parkland shooting meant two things for the State of Connecticut.

[51] Howard Fuller and Nina Rees, "Proof Positive That Charter Schools Are Better," May 12, 2017, newsweek.com.
[52] Emmeline Zhao, "Raw Numbers: Charter Students Are Graduating from College at Three to Five Times the National Average," July 30, 2017, the 74Million.org.

While Connecticut had some of the strictest gun control laws in the land, Parkland was not an issue of gun control for Connecticut. After the cowardly shooting of innocents by a man from his hotel balcony into the Mandalay Bay concert in Las Vegas in October 2017, which killed at least fifty-nine and injured 527, eliminating bump stocks that allow semiautomatic weapons to be fired as automatic weapons would be a good idea and do so with Godspeed. But the Parkland school shooting meant that we as parents and schools had failed to teach our students the Golden Rule and the value of life. The Golden Rule is to do unto others as you would have done unto you. The second is the value of life. You may not take another person's life. You must respect the life of the people around you. The value of life should be taught by parents and schools. Then perhaps young people would not murder their peers. It has since come out that the Parkland shooting at Marjory Stoneman School could have been prevented years before. It was political correctness in pursuing the narrow approach to the school-to-prison pipeline of reducing suspensions and expulsions of disruptive students that prevented removal of the shooter, Nikolas Cruz, from his peers. In accordance with the politically correct version of the school-to-prison pipeline, Obama-era policy tried to artificially reduce the number of students that were disciplined. To do that, one would massage the numbers and keep troubled students with the regular students.

The effort to reduce mass incarceration is misplaced when you try "to reduce racial 'disparities' in suspensions and expulsions… In many of these districts, the drive to 'get our numbers right' has produced disastrous results, with startling increases in both the number and severity of disciplinary offenses, including assaults and beatings of teachers and students.'"[53] As reported by *Miami New Times*: "Superintendent Robert Runcie's signature achievement in Broward [where the Marjory Stoneman School was located] reforming discipline to keep students accused of low-level crimes in school instead of

---

[53] Peter Kirsanow, Commission on Civil Rights, quoted in "Did Lax Obama-Era School-Discipline Policies Enable the Parkland Shooter," David French, *National Review,* March 2, 2018.

suspended, expelled, or behind bars. Critics argue the district's new approach under Runcie allowed dangerous students such as Cruz to go unnoticed by law enforcement."[54]

Nikolas Cruz was a troubled student who was able to avoid arrest for his previous conduct, thereby green-lighting him to buy his murder weapons and still be around his fellow students. That is the third lesson of the Parkland shooting. That is a bad learning environment. But this digresses from educational opportunity offered by public charters. Let's double the number of charters in Connecticut for instance to eighteen thousand students. Such a small move today would represent only be about 4 percent of the public school population, which would still be a testament to the power of the public unions to stand in the schoolhouse door and tell students of color that they may not enter.

---

[54] "After Parkland Broward Schools Superintendent Robert Runcie Battles the NRA and Local Critics," Brittany Shammas, April 24, 2018.

Chapter 12

Breaking the Chain of the School-to-Prison Pipeline

I WAS A JAG officer at the 4th JAG Detachment. (Actually, we had different detachments, but we referred to ourselves as the 4th and still do to this date with the 4th JAG Officers' Association.) As a young captain in the JAG, I would defend soldiers who were charged with using marijuana or cocaine. Marijuana, cocaine, heroin, and other mind-altering drugs are not consistent with the good order and discipline of the army, so if a urinalysis test of the soldier came back hot, then the Army Reserve would process the soldier for discharge. If the soldier did not want to be discharged, he or she could choose a JAG officer attorney to represent them and challenge the government's evidence. This is where captains and majors would come in. A key to a urinalysis test is the chain of custody of the urine sample. The government had to show that the urine given and the results tested were of the same soldier. Therefore, the urinalysis chain of custody ledger received significant attention from defense counsel. The chain of custody ledger would start out with a tester signing out a vial. Then the tester would escort the soldier to the bathroom where the soldier would provide a sample. The tester would return the vial to the holder of samples, and the tester and holder of samples would sign the form. Then when the samples were shipped to a private lab, the shipping company had to sign for custody of the box. When the box was received by the testing laboratory, that person had to sign and bring the samples to a refrigerator. When a scientist retrieved the box from the refrigerator to run the actual tests on the samples, that scientist had to sign the ledger.

As a defense attorney, one of the first places you would look to build a defense for your client would be at the chain of custody ledger to see whether there were any gaps or mistakes so that you can *break the chain*. If you break the chain, then the case is over because the government cannot connect a positive urinalysis result to your client. This is as it should be. We need to *break the chain* of the school-to-prison pipeline. And how we do that is to take the beginning of the pipeline out of the state's control. Then the pipeline is shut down because the state does not control the two ends of the pipe. If a student wishes to remain in the traditional public school, he or she can. In fact, in the City of New York, there are even public charter schools that are colocated in the same building with a traditional public school. This sharing of a building together has resulted in better scores for both the public charter and traditional public school. Each can make the other better through competition. There is room for both.

But how did we get to where opponents of school choice can effectively block school choice for our students? When the citizens of our great nation debated adopting the constitution after the Constitutional Convention of 1787, there were arguments for and against the design of the Constitution. An anti-Federalist piece by *Brutus* on November 29, 1787, *Essays IV and XVI*, set forth a real challenge to democracy and freedom: "It is not to be expected that a legislature will be found in any country that will not have some of its members, who will pursue their private ends, and for which they will sacrifice the public good. [Legislators] of this character are generally artful and designing, and frequently possess brilliant talents and abilities; they commonly act in concert, and agree to share the spoils of their country among them."[55]

And why does Connecticut lie prostrate before these statists and the NEA and AFT? "The smaller the society, the fewer will probably be the distinct parties and interests composing it; the fewer the distinct parties and interests the more frequently will a majority be found of the same party; and the smaller the number of individuals composing a majority, and the smaller the compass within which they are placed, the more easily will they concert and execute their plans of oppression."[56] (James Madison in *The Federalist Papers*)

The State of Connecticut lacks free will as its legislature has been run by statists for over forty years with intermittent Republican governors, during which time the statist could bide their time till there was a Democrat governor to continue their statist agenda. And here the statists persist in denying educational choice to the socioeconomically disadvantaged in our state generally, and high need, African-American, white, Hispanic, Asian, and other students specifically. How does this mesh with their pontifications and pledges after the deaths of George Floyd and Breonna Taylor to reduce structural racism? They should have taken the barriers to school choice down yesterday.

This entire collusion between the statists and the public unions does violence to the Connecticut Constitution, which states in Article 1, Section II, "All free governments are instituted for the benefit of the citizen." That means that everything that the governor and legislature does is supposed to benefit the average citizen and not a special class of citizen. If the legislature and governor are ensuring ranks of state employees paying dues to public unions but at the same time denying educational choice to our poorest, they have failed the law of our constitution, and they have failed at good government. Good government is defined by two things: "first, fidelity to the object of government, which is the happiness of the people; second, a knowledge of the means by which that object can be best attained."[57] And the hap-

---

[55] Ralph Ketcham, *The Anti-Federalist Papers and the Constitutional Convention Debates* (Signet Classics: New York, 1986), 347.

[56] James Madison, *The Federalist Papers*, No. 10, p. 83.

[57] James Madison, *The Federalist Papers*, No. 62, p. 380.

piness of the people is as citizens qua citizens and not as special interests. If special interests are happy, then somebody else's ox is probably being gored. In this instance, it is the innocents, our children.

Chapter 13

Prevailing Wage Further
Undermines Education

T HE OTHER LEG of the school-to-prison pipeline generally in America and specifically in Connecticut is something called prevailing wage. If a project in Connecticut is going to cost more than $650,000, a municipality is obligated to pay a higher rate of labor than otherwise available on the free market. That was the level that I learned of during my campaign. Effective October 31, 2017, the threshold was increased to $1,000,000 for new construction and $100,000 for renovation work.[58] There are prevailing wages also for federal work using federal appropriated funds and non-appropriated funds for blue-collar employees who are paid by the hour.[59] Instead of getting the low bidder to do the work, the pay must be done at a likely higher wage rate. While this is nice for the people actually doing the work, it means that the project costs more money for the school district at a time of deficit spending and infrastructure underspending. It is raw political power, contrary to ensuring the happiness of the people. It ensures the happiness of the few lucky workers on the projects.

---

[58] Connecticut Department of Labor, ctdol.state.ct.us.
[59] opm.gov.

It is like buying two for the price of three. And here again the statists have sold out our children for the cronies and allies of the statists.

If you feel that you are on the inside and that you or your family may be able to profit by your insider status, then this subornation of our constitutional system to the powerful may not concern you. But the majority of citizens should be concerned, and I would offer that the poor are not equally sited to profit from insider deals or higher wages to the friends of the statists. Instead, the schools in poorer districts are more likely to go with a broken boiler, leaking rooms, sometimes working bathrooms, and drafty windows longer as school districts in poorer areas end up spending money not just on their students but also on labor costs that are artificially inflated to reflect prevailing wages for the connected. Is this what progressive government looks like? Favors to the connected whilst our children are locked into schools that their parents or guardians may not want?

Usually, when we go to the supermarket, we try to buy three apples for the price of two. The prevailing wage for building new schools or renovating older schools, removing asbestos, sealing leaking roofs, and adding new classroom space requires that we only build two new schools for the price of three, or we only renovate two schools instead of three. This is nonsensical and exposes the power of those that seek to use their government power to benefit the few. Guess who gets shortchanged? Could it be schools in lower socio-economic neighborhoods? Yes. Cities in Connecticut like Hartford, Bridgeport, New Haven, and New Britain get a lot of their budgets from state injections of cash as they cannot raise enough money relying solely on their own property taxes and fees. In these environments, money is tight. That is a theme in general. Money is tight. With rising costs in municipal and state budgets to cover the underfunded pension and health care promises to retired workers, there is less and less to run the municipality or state.

Why is it good government to make it more expensive to renovate a school? This seems to only make sense to the Whole Foods crowd. As a frugal individual, I have occasionally gone into Whole Foods to see what the excitement is about, but I find myself unable to make many purchases because it is so much more expensive than at ShopRite. Compared to ShopRite, it is literally two items for what you would pay for three at Shoprite. On one occasion, I spoke with the black parking lot attendant about the fancy store that he was working for. He said, "I can't buy anything in there. It is too expensive." And there you have it. "Let them eat cake"—popularly attributed to Marie Antoinette upon learning that the peasants had no bread—seems to be the attitude of the statists.

Well, we can't afford prevailing wage. There is not enough money in the till. Not surprisingly, the attitude of college-educated whites in suburbs is not as strong on charter schools and vouchers as it is in black communities. So while the college-educated affluent have the choice of their own decently financed public school or have the ability to send their children to a private school or afford a religious school like a Catholic day school, they deny real choices for primarily black and Latino children to have an effective choice beyond their own local public school. Perhaps this attitude comes from what they have "learned" from their local school union and board of education or the progressive newspapers in their communities. Just don't ask the black and Latino residents of educationally challenged communities what they would like to do. These affluent suburbanites don't have the time to listen. They are also busy buying two items for the price of three at Whole Foods and are not entirely clear on why urban schools can't just pay for new schools or renovations at the inflated price of prevailing wage. Doesn't everyone eat organic food?

Chapter 14

We Can Do Better

S O WHAT COMES out at the end of the school-to-prison pipe-line so well maintained by the state? People who go to jail. It's a result that we all want to avoid, Republicans, Democrats, and unaffiliated voters. In one of my meetings with the gentleman from the NAACP debate, who had spent years in jail, he shared a letter from his father with me. His father had been incarcerated in Connecticut for much of the man's formative years. The letter was written in a beautiful script that was not learned in school as it was so artistic. The script was almost like one of those handwritten invitations for a wedding because they looked so much better than regular script.

His father wrote his heartfelt sentiments so much better than I could write myself. It was a letter written to the parole board seeking an early release. He basically conveyed the sentiment that he was resigned to the fact that as a black man in America, he was required to be processed and catalogued by the state. That he would be incarcerated at some point in his life was also an accepted fact. This he accepted as his fate, but could the parole board have some leniency? This was never my assumption as an immigrant from Germany to this great country, nor was it the assumption of most of my classmates at Greenwich High School, nor, I speculate, is it the future assumed by most students in school today in America. But this man's father ended up at the end of the pipeline that lead to jail. How did he get there, and what can be done to make it less likely to be repeated? This book is much too small to get at many of the reasons and changes that could be made. My subsequent book on *The Chicago Tragedy and the 100 Questions after the Killing of George Floyd and Breonna Taylor with Policy Recommendations*, attempts in part, to look at a better way. But when you look at the incarceration rate for young black men versus the general population, it is jarring. According to a report, black men in their twenties and early thirties without a high school diploma had an incarceration rate at some point in their life of 40 percent.[60] This ends up having a disparate impact on black women who live in the same communities, as there are fewer men around to date, marry, and raise families together with. This leads to fewer children, boys and girls, that have fathers present in their lives to help raise them and set examples for them. And we know that children with both parents in the home do better emotionally, mentally, physically, and academically than households where one or both parents are missing. There is necessarily a higher crime rate for men raised in homes without a father present. It is a self-perpetuating process. As pointed out in the report by Secretary of Housing and Urban Development Patrick Moynihan, *The Negro Family, the case for National Action* in 1965, the number of families where no man was present in the black community had risen from one-third to two-thirds from 1935 to 1965, a *doubling* during the War on Poverty, a.k.a. the War on the Family. A ten-year-old boy does not want to be a tough guy and end up in jail by eighteen or twenty-two years of age or in a pinewood box, but how do we change that trajectory if the state keeps the pipeline open?

But the statists insist that the pipeline stay open! These self-same statists fight to keep control of the schools. The statists issue press releases and have interviews where they say that they are the

---

[60] "Incarceration Rate for African-Americans now six times the national average," rt.com, February 20, 2013.

champions of the downtrodden. But the Chavistas in Venezuela are constantly saying that they are fighting for the poor and against the capitalists and the counter-revolutionaries while they drive what was previously one of the richest countries in South America, Venezuela, with the largest proven oil reserves in the western hemisphere, into abject poverty. Over 80 percent of the country was malnourished by 2019. Basic medical supplies were also unavailable. There were constant rolling blackouts that the Chavistas blamed on the Yanquis from America to the Venezuelan analog and antiquated electrical system. The last thing the Chavistas will do is relinquish control. Some people believe the Chavistas regret devastating the economy, but these onlookers forget that starvation is one of the principal tools of socialists to gain and keep control of their countries. If you spend hours and hours in line just to get some food and you are constantly hungry, you have little energy or time to push back against the well-fed military and statists. Every time the Chavistas in Venezuela crow that they are fighting against the revanchists and for the poor, they buckle down even more on the citizenry. Likewise, the NEA and AFT claim that they are for the children, yet they are invigorated by blocking public charter schools as well as voucher programs for high-needs children who would be better able to choose to go to a private school or Catholic school with the aid of such a voucher. These high-needs children would actually have a previously unavailable choice. The NEA and AFT order of priorities is first to union members, then to the union, and then in third place are our children, the students. Our children are third in line when they should be first! But these progressives and statists will fight diligently against competition and actual school choice for economically disadvantaged communities. The analogy to the Chavistas in Venezuela is telling as they would rather the schools atrophy under state and union control than more choices be offered to the economically disadvantaged.

Chapter 15

COVID-19 Bares Some Truths

R EPORTS OF A coronavirus epidemic striking in Wuhan, China, started to circulate in January 2020. But that was over there. We were over here. Why worry? It is so far away. Then cases started to appear in Italy and Spain and elsewhere and then in the United States. But we shouldn't be alarmed. Nonetheless, on January 31, 2019, the Trump administration put limits on the ability of non-Americans from China to fly to the United States. American citizens still could. The same was done later regarding Europe, but they still allowed flights for Americans to go back and forth, so the virus could still spread. Nonetheless, the travel ban on China-originated flights was seen by some as too draconian.[61] Speaker Nancy Pelosi took an opportunity on February 24, 2020, to walk through Chinatown in San Francisco to support the commercial district and say that it was safe to go there. "The speaker said there's no reason for people to live in fear."[62] A month later, on the other side of the nation, Mayor Bill de Blasio wanted to calm nerves and texted in early March 2020

---

[61] Ethan Epstein, "Trump never actually banned flights from China or Europe. Why?" *The Washington Times*, March 22, 2020.

[62] David Louie, "Coronavirus concerns: Speaker Pelosi tours San Francisco's Chinatown to show it's safe," ABC7, February 24, 2020.

that people should "go on with your lives + get out on the town despite Coronavirus."[63] Hindsight is always twenty-twenty. I would not trade places with any mayor, governor, or other chief executive who had to make decisions on how to proceed with this COVID-19 virus. It was new, and we in America had not had a virus like this in a century. There had been viruses in Asia and in Africa, but they were generally snuffed out and extinguished before they became a significant problem in the Americas or Europe. Not this time.

Back during the Great Recession, at the beginning of the presidential administration of Barack Obama, Rahm Emanuel, who was the twenty-third White House chief of staff from 2009 to 2010, was quoted as saying that during a time of crisis, "[y]ou never let a serious crisis go to waste. And what I mean by that it's an opportunity to do things you think you could not do before."[64] It is not an overstatement to say that public unions and statists are not ambivalent about public charter schools in Connecticut. They would rather there be fewer educational choices for high-needs children and, by extension, fewer public charter schools. How do the opponents of public charter schools, which serve primarily African American and Hispanic students in Connecticut and beyond Connecticut, succeed in suppressing those schools that exist and preventing more from being created? It helps when the opponents of school choice have worked diligently through donations and campaign volunteers to elect politicians who oppose public charter schools and vouchers. These self-same politicians return the favor by militating against public charter schools and vouchers.

The introduction of COVID-19 to America in 2020 proved to be an opportunity for the opponents of school choice to use the crises for their own objectives. Overlapping the COVID-19 epidemic were protests following the killing of African American George Floyd in Minneapolis, Minnesota, and the killing of African American Breonna Taylor in Louisville, Kentucky. While the leaders

---

[63] Madison Dibble, "De Blasio haunted by weeks-old tweet urging people to 'get out on the town despite coronavirus,'" *The Washington Examiner*, March 25, 2020.

[64] Rahm Emmanuel Quotes, BrainyQuote.com.

of the public unions might have expressed support for the protestors
and for Black Lives Matter, they at the same time were working to
squelch public charter schools that serve primarily African American
students in New York City, Connecticut, and elsewhere. But we are
not supposed to discuss their hypocrisy.

When the coronavirus hit, it became apparent that the transmission was somehow through the air or through touching the same
thing as an infected person, maybe touching your eyes or nose, or
maybe breathing the air that an infected person had exhaled or
sneezed out. We still don't know enough about the virus. How to
avoid getting the virus? Social distancing. Stay six feet away. Wear
a mask. Close restaurants and bars. Close schools. Close businesses.
Work from home. Reduce your exposure to others. Increase testing. Then positive test results were coming in for people with only
a background trace of COVID-19 that may not even have made the
person sick, thereby exaggerating its reach. The young appeared to
be considerably less vulnerable. One estimate in October 2020 said
that old people were one thousand times more likely to die from
COVID-19 than young people. People with diabetes, obesity, and
high blood pressure were at higher risk of falling seriously ill or dying
from the virus. States like Connecticut, New York, California, and
Michigan, which pursued stricter shutdowns of businesses, ended
up with greater economic declines in the second quarter of 2020.
Earnings dropped for the states with more severe restrictions: New
York (-36.8 percent), New Jersey (-31.5 percent), California (-30.8
percent) and Connecticut (-29 percent).[65] Other states that did not
close down as strictly suffered less of an income decline like Utah
(-14 percent), Arizona (-18.1 percent), Texas (-21.6 percent), and
Florida (-22.3 percent).[66] This extended to unemployment rates that
remained higher in the higher restriction states like New York (12.5
percent), California (11.4 percent), Illinois (11 percent), New Jersey
(10.9 percent), Washington (8.5 percent), Connecticut (8.1 percent

---

[65] "United States Bureau of Economic Analysis, second-quarter state personal
income report," September 2020, cited in "Congress's Coiid Income
Redistribution," *Wall Street Journal*, September 29, 2020, p. A16.

[66] Id.

), and Oregon (7.7 percent). States that did not pursue as extensive a shutdown had lower unemployment rates, such as Utah (4.1 percent), Georgia (5.6 percent), Arizona (5.9 percent), Indiana (6.4 percent), Texas (6.8 percent), and Florida (7.4 percent).[67]

Two thousand and twenty indeed brought unsettling times with economic dislocations from the coronavirus as well as the demonstrations over the killing of George Floyd, which were sometimes hijacked by outside groups who had their own agenda and turned otherwise peaceful protests to petition the government for redress of grievances into violent riots that destroyed property and closed businesses. It got so bad in some cities that white liberals could literally put a Black Lives Matter T-shirt on and go into a black neighborhood and burn it down, all the while boasting about how much they cared about the black community. In the meantime, they had destroyed black-owned businesses that had taken years to build up. They had destroyed businesses that were owned by other Americans that had taken years of blood, sweat, and tears to build up. These protestors destroyed the jobs where many blacks worked. In addition, by going after stores like Walmart and the like, they attempted to recreate food deserts where fresh fruits and vegetables were not as readily available for a better diet for those living in these high-needs neighborhoods. This is what "allies" of the black community do, and they are lauded for it. Something is wrong. Or how about the white woman telling a black woman over fifty years old, who was wearing a Black Lives Matter T-shirt, "She was not black enough to be wearing that T-shirt." Where do these people come from?

These may be of the same sort that stand in the schoolhouse door with Governor George Wallace, and they tell black and Hispanic children that they may not enter the public charter school. They equally block black and Hispanic children from other schools by denying vouchers to high-needs children. So who are these people who stand with George Wallace to prevent more school choice? Who are these people who have tried to use the crisis of the coronavirus to dismantle and hamstring public charter schools that primarily

---

[67] Id.

serve high-needs black, Hispanic, white, Asian, and other children in many cities and states?

With the advent of COVID-19, we were learning how to respond to the novel coronavirus. We went from encouraging people to come and shop in Chinatown in San Francisco to going out on the town in New York City to see a movie and entertain yourself to shutdowns in a few short weeks. Again, no mayor, governor, chief executive officer, or president can be faulted for how they responded or that they acted in bad faith. They responded as they saw appropriate with their information and their political instincts for what was best. Some were more willing to use state power to stop the free actions of citizens than others. February moved to March, and things accelerated in the middle of March to the cancellation of school and, within ten days' time, the shutting down of the entire ski industry. Whilst an outlier for many, consider that skiing is done outside. The lifts that people ride are outside. Mountains could still operate without their gondola cars where people ride together in an enclosed space. Dining facilities could be shut down, but the entire industry shut down due to concerns about "what if?" What if this new virus spreads rapidly? What if your workers get the virus even though most of them are outside? This is in the interest of protecting customers and staff. Like many businesses, the ski industry went down their options and found that shutting down was the rational choice, as did a number of businesses. Then restaurants were shut down for in-restaurant dining. Takeout food could still be had, although we still did not have a sense of whether the physical touching of the paper bag by a restaurant worker could lead to the infection of a customer by touching the bag. We now know better that touching is less likely to cause transmission. More likely is being in an enclosed space with an infected person who is breathing out a lot of these coronavirus droplets. It seems that not just one or two bits of the virus can infect you. Rather, a high viral load is usually necessary. But we are still learning about this virus, and we will have to learn to live with it for the rest of our lives.

With businesses shutting down and schools being shut down to avoid interaction amongst citizens, existing Internet businesses like Zoom video conferencing took off. You may be familiar with FaceTime where you can speak with someone else whilst looking at video of the other person in real time on your iPhone. Your Samsung or Android phone should allow you to Skype or do something called Google Hangouts. There is even an app called Viber. At all events, if you have a smartphone, you can talk to someone and see their face on your phone. These types of applications would allow people to continue to work but to do so at home. If a worker did not come to the office, then no disease could be transmitted, and that worker would still be available to work for the company. Jokes then abounded of people on Zoom conferences with many people, with a nice shirt or blouse on. But then when the conference was over, the person got up and merely had pajama pants on. For the new pajama crowd, they could stay at home but still do their work and get paid. This was an excellent example of how technology could help our nation continue working in the face of the coronavirus.

But not all workers could take advantage of this technology. If you were a frontline worker and work in the food industry or retail, you have to interact with the customer. That means answering questions and checking out their purchase at the register. Even for takeout food, the customer and restaurant necessarily had to be in close proximity with this disease with unknown capabilities. Partly because blacks and Hispanics had a higher percentage of frontline work that could not be done at a remote distance, these citizens were also infected at a higher rate, not to mention closer living quarters with some multigenerational situations at home that put the older family members at greater risk from exposure to the younger family members who came back from frontline work. If you were in the health care industry, you still had to take care of sick patients.

Nonetheless, remote work was a panacea for many. Some of the well-to-do were able to decamp from their urban housing in places like New York City and head to their second homes and work from there. Other well-to-do citizens had the financial wherewithal to rent short- and long-term homes in the suburbs of New York, for instance, to ride out the first wave of the coronavirus in a sequestered environment. There was even the ability to teach students remotely via computers. This might sound like a nice solution. It has, however, proven to be much more complicated in practice. Preliminarily high-needs communities tended to have fewer laptop or desktop computers to use, let alone a reliable Internet connection. Or if there was a computer or laptop, there might have been more than one child in the home.

Even in the best of circumstances, it would be fair to say that most public and private school systems were not prepared to go to online learning in a few weeks' time. Teachers were not trained to do it. Teachers did not have a curriculum prepared for online learning, and the schools did not necessarily have uniform facilities for all their teachers to convey their lessons, tests, and homework to their students. But all was not lost. There were actually some online public charter schools in the nation. That is an incredible coincidence. Who would have thought of online teaching for children and families that need that option? Normally, one would have thought that school districts would have come running to these online schools to learn how they did it since they already pioneered online teaching for K-12.

But not all is as it should be. If a politician is dead-set against the expansion of school choice for our children, then that politician might use any excuse to eliminate school choice. That was the action of Governor Kate Brown of Oregon in the throes of the coronavirus in March 2020. On March 12, 2020, Governor Brown directed public schools to remain closed statewide from March 16 through March 31, 2020. It is one thing to shut public schools so that students and teachers don't interact and infect each other, but it is quite another thing to go out of your way to shut online charter schools! How does that make sense?

On March 17, 2020, Governor Brown issued Executive Order no. 20-08. In the order, *public schools* were defined to include "schools within a school district, educational service district, or public charter."[68] With the new order, schools would remain closed through April 28, 2020, and this would include all public charter schools.

---

[68] Executive Order No. 20-08, Office of the Governor, State of Oregon, para. 1, March 17, 2020.

"[P]ublic schools that close pursuant to paragraph 2 of this Executive Order for the closure period shall continue to receive allocations from the State School Fund, as if they had been actually in session during the closure period."[69] On its surface, it does not appear to single out online public charter schools, but it did mean that "online schools, perfectly designed to protect students, had to shut down too."[70] According to former state representative Jeff Kropf, an online charter school that he was working with in March had taken on three hundred new students earlier but had another 1,600 waiting to get in, but those numbers had to be approved by the director of the Oregon Department of Education, Colt Gill. "Teachers unions know that if parents and students get a taste of the high quality and safety of online schooling…they might not come back. And if they stay away…so do the dollar signs attached to each of your kids."[71]

In a report on April 6, 2020, Reverend Ben Johnson reported that "state officials confirmed that the 13,000 students enrolled in those schools are needlessly sitting idle so that community public schools can maintain their funding levels."[72] The article went on to quote Marc Siegel, spokesman for the Oregon Department of Education, that "Executive Order 20-08 closed all public schools, including virtual charter schools."[73] It is a logic that can only make sense in the *Kafkaesque* world of statists.

> Franz Kafka's…surreal fiction vividly expressed the anxiety, alienation and powerlessness of the individual in the 20th century. Kafka's work is characterized by nightmarish settings in which characters are crushed by nonsensical, blind authority, Thus, the word *Kafkaesque* is often

---

[69] Id., para. 3.

[70] "Gov. Brown needlessly shuts down online charter schools," OregonWatchdog. com, March 27, 2020, quoting Lars Larson.

[71] Id.

[72] "13,000 children are being denied an education over a funding fight," Action Institute Powerblog, April 6, 2020.

[73] Id.

applied to bizarre and impersonal administrative situations where the individual feels powerless to understand or control what is happening.[74]

How would you explain the shutting of online schools during a pandemic to an adult, let alone a child in the school? You cannot, other than to say that this is the power of the AFT and NEA for the teacher unions to protect the jobs of their members at the expense of children. True, online schools were still authorized to do "supplemental work" just as other public schools could do at home, but the online schools could not teach their normal curriculum. Supplemental work is basically there to keep students busy during the shutdown and is not graded.

Furthermore, the "[e]nrollment of new students to virtual public charter schools during the closure would impact school funding for districts across Oregon and therefore may impact the distribution of state school funds and delivery of services."[75] In the words of the Action Institute, the state was "denying thousands of Oregon's students an education, to keep taxpayer money flowing to the inflexible and union-dominated traditional school system."[76] If a citizen is left scratching his or her head at these power politics, Action Institute quoted President Franklin Delano Roosevelt, the thirty-second president of the United States, on militant labor tactics against the citizens who pay their bills as "unthinkable and intolerable." The NEA and FTA are so strong across our country that there is little that we can do, until the politicians from all parties put our children first in a fairer and more equitable educational environment.

The sometimes uttered "truth to power" phrase is inapplicable to the muscular AFT and NEA. Few civil rights leaders have been willing to challenge the denial of school choice to high-needs black, Hispanic, white, Asian, and other students as practiced and encour-

---

[74] "*Kafkaesque* Literature," *Merriam-Webster*, merriam-webster.com, accessed September 29, 2020.

[75] Oregon Department of Education's guidance to school districts, quoted in "13,000 children are being denied an education over a funding fight."

[76] "13,000 children are being denied an education over a funding fight."

aged by the NEA and AFT. "Truth to power," "good trouble," and "wokeness" do not apply!

At what point should the state be able to prevent children from enrolling in an online public charter school? In April 2020, if one tried to enroll in Oregon Connections Academy public charter school, a message would come up: "Due to Governor Brown's Executive Order 20-08, as of March 27, 2020, the Oregon Department of Education has advised that no students are able to withdraw or enroll in any schools during the school closure."[77] By protecting the brick-and-mortar schools from losing students to online schools, is that fair to a parent or guardian's right to choose what is best for their children? As the pandemic continued through the summer of 2020 and on into the fall, the Oregon Department of Education sharpened its limits on online charter schools to further appease the public education unions. In 2020, Oregon had twenty virtual public charter schools, which enrolled about thirteen thousand students. The state intentionally imposed limits to their expansion during the pandemic. These schools had been operating for more than fifteen years. Clearly they had figured out how to teach online and satisfy the Oregon Department of Education. For all the public exhortations of protecting our children during the pandemic by school officials, if a parent or guardian decided that online learning might be the better route in the fall, the state was more interested in protecting the jobs of teachers in traditional schools than the education of our children. In 2011, the statists had already put a 3 percent cap in how many students in an Oregon school district could enroll in a virtual public charter school. Therefore, if a district in Oregon was already at 3 percent, the district could deny new enrollments "and provide other online options." As of August 7, 2020, ten school districts had already hit their 3 percent cap. Apply, get denied, and then appeal to the State Board of Education. That doesn't seem to be an efficient way to give your children school choice. And although a bill had been submitted to raise the cap in June 2020, it wasn't on the list of bills for a spe-

---

[77] "Our view: Should Oregon block enrollment in online schools?," easternoregonian.com/opinion/editorials, April 8, 2020.

cial session of the legislature in August 2020.[78] Online schooling was appealing to some parents and guardians as a safer route during the pandemic, but that route was blocked by the allies of the AFT and NEA.

The marionettes of the AFT and NEA in the Oregon Department of Education, however, were not through delivering the goods to their puppet masters. As the summer of 2020 wore on toward the fall, the question by parents, guardians, and boards of education were whether in-person schooling might be available to their children in the fall of 2020. More restrictions and guidances were issued by the Oregon Department of Education over the summer. If certain COVID-19 infection numbers were hit or missed, plus other requirements a school system could or could not open. Nonetheless, more clarifications were issued in July and August of 2020 until there appeared to be some light in the sky that maybe some children might actually be able to go back to school with their peers. Small school districts that served small populations of fewer than seventy-five students would be able to work with local health authorities to see how they could reopen.[79] Great. So now at least a small school system could open. But no. The enforcers of the NEA and AFT clarified that the Hermiston Christian School, a K-12 school in Hermiston, Oregon, with a student body of fifty-one students, could not reopen.[80] Don't worry. If you fight to keep your school open and give education choice to your students, you may only be fined up to $1,250 and imprisoned up to thirty days. Is that per student? Is that per day? For how long can the state lock a teacher or administrator up, and how quickly can they bankrupt a private school fighting to

---

[78] Natalie Pate, "Older law could prevent students from switching to virtual charter schools during Covid-19," *Salem Statesman Journal*, August 7, 2020, updated August 8, 2020.

[79] Nik Streng, "New ODE guidance gives further exemptions for rural and remote schools," *The Argus Observer*, August 12, 2020, accessed October 29, 2020.

[80] Jon Brown (no relation to Oregon Governor Kate Brown), "Small Christian School Sues Oregon Governor for Shutting Private Religious Schools While Letting Public Schools Reopen," DailyWire.com, October 21, 2020, accessed October 26, 2020.

survive during the COVID-19 pandemic? A subsequent lawsuit by the Hermiston Christian School in October 2019 quoted a policy advisor and liaison for Oregon Governor Brown as saying there was a "potential for a 'mass exodus' of children from public schools and emphasized that public schools could suffer a reduction in funding if students disenrolled to obtain education elsewhere."[81]

"There is no legitimate reason for allowing public schools with 75 or fewer students to provide in-person instruction while denying the same opportunity to small private schools, including religious ones."[82] And so the NEA and AFT juggernaut rolls through our education system, flattening anyone bold enough to stand up for our children.

Lest one think that legislative action or inaction, executive action or inaction are the only ways to diminish school choice for black, Hispanic, white, Asian, or other students from high-needs neighborhoods, starving public charters of public funds is another tool of the opponents of school choice to diminish school choice.

---

[81] Id.

[82] Ryan Tucker, The Alliance Defending Freedom senior counsel, quoted in "Small Christian School Sues Oregon Governor."

Chapter 16

Defunding the Education of High-Needs Students

A FTER THE KILLING of George Floyd in May 2020 in Minneapolis, Minnesota, protests erupted in cities and towns across the United States. They even sparked some protests outside of the United States. The term *Black Lives Matter* became a household word. Black Lives Matter signs showed up in people's yards, and Black Lives Matter T-shirts could be spotted in many communities. One of the policy proposals of the demonstrators was for accountability by the police. This meant that a few bad apples should not be allowed to potentially harm their communities, in general, and the African American community specifically. This would mean that there could be greater access to disciplinary records of police officers and that problem officers could either be retrained or removed from police work. Accountability was to make police accountable to the citizen. Collective bargaining agreements, however, can make accountability a tall order as there are confidentially rules and arbitration procedures to protect the interests of the police, for better or worse. These collective bargaining agreements could not be reworked overnight. Another policy that some demonstrators promoted was to "defund the police."

The more famous move to defund the police was in the city where George Floyd was killed—Minneapolis, Minnesota. Minneapolis City Council president Lisa Bender was quoted as saying, "We are committed to dismantling policing as we know it [in] the city of Minneapolis and to rebuild within our community a new model of public safety that actually keeps our community safe."[83] According to CNN, Ms. Bender had another eight members on the council on board to defund the police department out of a total of twelve members, a clear majority. The idea of defunding police departments sounded then and sounds today as unrealistic. When crime is an everyday reality in some communities, the only people who can stop the criminals in the first instance are police. Whether society can address poverty, broken families, mental illness, housing shortages, drug addiction, domestic abuse, etc. is a discussion to be held at the same time, but abolishing a police department puts the citizens who need the protection the most from the police at risk. Ms. Bender said, "[We need] to listen, especially to our black leaders, to our communities of color, for whom policing is not working and to really let the solutions lie in our community."[84]

This pledge to defund the police was two weeks after the killing of George Floyd. *The Washington Post* quoted a city council member as saying that the council is "taking immediate steps toward ending" the force.[85] By the end of September 2020, the reality was that there would be no defunding of the police department in Minneapolis. According to a poll by the Minneapolis *Star Tribune*, cited by *The New York Times*, 50 percent of black residents opposed reducing the size of the police department.[86] The city council did pass a provision to ask voters to take the police department from the city's charter and

---

[83] Christina Maxouris and Josh Campbell, "Minneapolis City Council members intend to defund and dismantle the city's police department," Dakin and one, cnn.com, June 8, 2020.
[84] Id.
[85] "9 Minneapolis City Council members announce plans to disband police department," washingtonpost.com, June 8, 2020.
[86] Astead W. Herndon, "How a Pledge to Dismantle the Minneapolis Police Collapsed," *The New York Times*, nytimes.com, September 26, 2020.

put public safety duties under a new department. This was turned down, 10-5, by the Minneapolis Charter Commission, which called for further study.[87]

However one might feel about defunding a police department, it is likely that even fewer people support defunding schools. How about defunding schools that teach primarily black and Hispanic children from high-needs communities? Does that sound like a good idea? No. It does not. But that is what is happening in Connecticut and may be happening in your state. The defunding of public charter schools is being enabled and supported by many of the same people who scaled their soapbox after the killing of George Floyd and Breonna Taylor to say that they would work for racial justice, racial equality, and against something called structural racism, which lacks a coherent definition or accounting of just what structural racism is.[88] These same political and business leaders pledged themselves to work for the betterment and amelioration of conditions in the African American community. Yet these self-same people stand in the

---

[87] Id.

[88] It is likely that if what comports "structural racism" were written in a circle on a Venn diagram and that which comports "structural statism" were written in a circle on a Venn diagram, the two circles would share much more in common than what would fall outside of their identical contents. Structural racism and structural statism are almost the same. Structural statism is a variant of statism. "Statism" as defined by en.m.wikipedia.org, in political science is the doctrine that the political authority of the state is legitimate to some degree. Wikipedia continued that "[s]tatism can take many forms from small government to big government. "The ideology of statism holds that sovereignty in not vested in the people, but in the nation state and that all individuals and associations exist only to enhance the power, prestige and well-being of the state." Statism is diametrically opposed to the foundation of our great nation in the Declaration of Independence that the citizen is sovereign and that we are not be ruled by our "betters": "We hold these Truths to be self-evident, that all Men are created equal, that they are endowed by their Creator with certain unalienable Rights, that among these are Life, Liberty, and the Pursuit of Happiness. That to secure these Rights, Governments are instituted among Men, deriving *their just powers from the Consent of the Governed,* that whenever any Form of Government become destructive of these Ends, it is the Right of the People to alter or to abolish it, and to institute new Government." (emphasis added)

schoolhouse door and tell African American and Hispanic children that they may not enter the public charter schools. These political and business leaders achieve this by working against the expansion of the number of public charter schools or place caps on the ability of existing public charter schools to add more grades or more students in each grade.

Why would these politicians and business leaders talk out of one side of their mouth and do the opposite? Some might say because they are good politicians and business leaders. "Don't look at what I do, listen to what I say." Yet the forces opposing expanded school choice for high-needs blacks and Hispanics stand resolutely in the way of public charter schools. In Connecticut, the money follows the student to some degree. The state of Connecticut gives a set amount to the public charter school per student. For four years prior to 2018, the funding in Connecticut had been $11,000 per student. Two hundred and fifty dollars was finally added in 2018. That amounts to a mere .0227 increase in five years. A newsflash to the enemies of school choice: things get more expensive every year. Electricity and some energy bills increase. Teachers' costs for rent, mortgage, cars, food, and clothes increase over five years. How are you supposed to keep a staff of motivated teachers if you cannot increase their wage? How can public charters pay utilities and maintenance on their buildings when the state only gives them a paltry increase after five years? This parsimonious funding is not by accident but rather an effort to defund schools that serve primarily black and Hispanic students. The architects of the school-to-prison pipeline want each and every one of these students back in the public union-run schools. By bringing ten thousand students back, there would be more teachers hired in the public union-run schools, and more dues would be sent to the AFT and NEA and their headquarters in Washington, DC. In May 2018, 70 percent of the students in Connecticut's charters schools came from low-income households, and eight in ten students were black or Hispanic.[89]

---

[89] Danielle Capalbo, ConnCan.org, May 18, 2018.

In 2019, Dacia Toll, a co-CEO of the charter organization Achievement First, said they had to economize due to being short-changed by the state to cut teaching positions, cut budgets, field trips, after-school programs, and teacher coaching.[90] Toll said that many traditional public schools serving the same types of students with higher economic needs get thousands more through state and local funding.[91] While it is true that localities will help with transportation of the students to a public charter and to recompense for the costs of special education students, these public charters are short-changed. They should be getting $15,000 to $16,000 per student. In the report in the CT Mirror, expenditures per student of $14,697 per Bridgeport public student was cited $19,837 for Hartford and $18,064 for New Haven. New York City was reported to give $6,000 more in state and local funding per student than Connecticut. Rhode Island gave about $3,600 more per student according to Ms. Toll and the CT Mirror report.[92]

Money had been so tight that Achievement First had to make staff reductions every year for the four years previous to 2019 in all its Connecticut schools. They even had to consolidate two Hartford schools by moving their Summit Middle School into the Hartford Academy Middle School.[93] This would be alarming on its own, but when the performance of Achievement First is considered along with its peers in the traditional public schools, it is alarming. Wouldn't the politicians see better results and direct more resources in the direction of a successful program? That would be too idealistic. According to Achievement First, on a percentage of student body basis, more than twice as many students performed at grade level on the state's standardized tests compared to the host district students attending neighborhood schools.[94] "In 2017, Achievement First Amistad High School was ranked first among high schools in the state by U.S. News

---

[90] Kathleen Megan, "Charter Schools 'literally starving' for state funds says school leader," CtMirror.org, November 7, 2019.

[91] Id.

[92] Id.

[93] Id.

[94] Id.

& World Report; [in 2019] Achievement First Hartford High School was ranked Number 3."[95]

Who is working to defund these schools? Even if they only performed at the same level as their neighboring traditional public schools, that alone would be enough to keep them in business with equal funding since the parents and guardians had made the decision that it was a better environment for their children. No bureaucrat may interject themselves and claim to know what is better for these parents' and guardians' children and work diligently to foreclose this avenue.

But the enemies of school choice for black and Hispanic children are legion, all the while claiming that they are the true champions of the powerless. How long have you been in power, and what do you have to show for it? Did levels of education and high school graduation rates increase or decrease during your tenure? Have the rates of high school graduates graduating from a four-year degree program within six years increased or decreased? Are the levels of unemployment for your graduates higher or lower? In speaking to Education Secretary Betsy DeVos at a budget hearing, Connecticut Congresswoman Rosa DeLauro stated the following: "In my view, this budget is full of cruel cuts to education programs and it baffles me that you found room for a $60 million increase to the charter school programs…especially when you consider recent reports of waste and abuse in that program."[96]

That is an example of a blanket opposition to public charter schools, regardless if any of that money were coming to public charter schools in Connecticut, which are underfunded. Should one expect more than a knee-jerk response to helping public charter schools from a committed statist? The waste and abuse that Congressman DeLauro was referring to related to charters which received monies and never opened in other states or the nepotism of granting contracts to family members, which would seem to be an obvious no-no if they are no-bid contracts.

---

[95]   Id.

[96]   Peter Urban, "DeLauro Slams Proposed Funding Increase for Charter Schools," *CT News Junkie*, March 29, 2019.

Public charters that do well deserve support. Congresswoman DeLauro is an enthusiastic opponent of school choice for black, Hispanic, white, Asian, and other students from high-needs families. Otherwise, she would have distinguished between aid to problematic charters and successful ones. How about successful ones in Connecticut? Or should no public charter school receive accolades from her regardless of exemplary results? "Cruel" and "reckless" make for a headline-grabbing sound bite, but it is cruel and reckless to paint all charters as unworthy, particularly when you have stellar performers in Connecticut such as Stamford Charter School for Excellence. The children don't matter to a statist, only the retention or aggrandizement of power by the state and its allies.

Connecticut State Senator Julie Kushner unleashed an attack on public charter schools in the Danbury Democratic Town Committee site in August 2020: "Some claim a charter school is a magic bullet. This is not accurate. A charter school would drain much-need funds from our school budget. Danbury schools would lose state funding for students enrolled in the charter."[97] It appears to be black and white to this state legislator. Public charter schools are not offered as a panacea but as an addition to a wide variety of educational options for our young, in addition to traditional public schools and vouchers which help high-needs families consider sending their children to a private school. If there are a paltry ten thousand students in Connecticut's public charter schools and over six thousand on wait-lists, it behooves the state to increase the number of seats by six thousand immediately so that these students can exercise their choice. In the myopic view of some, "[a] charter school would intensify our existing problems and would only be available to a small and select number of Danbury's students."[98] Where is the push for excellence? Where is the dreaming? Why should this small number of Danbury students go without? Why not make more public charter school seats available to Danbury students?

---

[97] "Charter Schools Are Not a Magic Bullet," danburydemocrats.com, August 18, 2020.
[98] State Senator Julie Kushner, Id.

Senator Kushner continued that "[o]ur top priority should be to ensure equitable opportunity. We must strive to reduce disparities and improve test scores, graduation rates, and college readiness among all students."[99] As discussed above, these are precisely where charters excel. Perhaps Senator Kushner is aware that the AFT and NEA will not abide the increase of public charter schools and choice in Connecticut if it can be prevented, so that she is not able to embrace these proven incubators of improved test scores, graduation rates from high school, college readiness, and graduation rates from four-year colleges in six years. Would this senator's opposition to public charters also include the effort to defund public charter schools for blacks and Hispanics?

---

[99] Id.

Chapter 17

How the AFT and NEA Work against School Choice for Black and Hispanic Students

I T IS ACCURATE to say that the expansion of public charter schools threatens to lessen the ranks of dues-paying members of the AFT and NEA as most, but not all, public charter schools are not unionized. Whether this helps or hinders the public charters' academic success of their students is not treated here. It is a truism that the greater the amount of school choice is granted to high-needs students by including more public charter school in the mix of traditional neighborhood schools, magnet schools, and vouchers, the fewer members there will be of the AFT and NEA, if only incrementally. This runs counter to the desire for any organization to thrive and prosper and not idle and possibly contract. For that reason, the reasons given by the AFT and the NEA against public charter schools should be taken with a grain of salt as the motivation for public charter schools is to benefit our children, who are our future, and the motivation for the AFT and NEA is to squash all newcomers, otherwise the AFT and NEA risk shrinking as teachers migrate from traditional schools to different teaching opportunities.

Public charter schools are no longer newcomers in that they have been around for over twenty-five years. In 2017, the NEA adopted a new charter school position to replace their last NEA-approved charter school policy in 2001.[100] In the words of the NEA press release: "The new NEA Policy Statement on Charter Schools will boost NEA's *forceful support* of state and local efforts *to limit* charter growth and increase charter accountability, and slow the diversion of resources from neighborhood public schools to charters."[101]

In the view of the NEA, the number of charters had risen so dramatically that it exceeded the ability of state and school districts to hold the public charters accountable. We learn from the NEA that the "growth of [public] charters has undermined local public schools and communities, without producing any overall increase in student learning and growth."[102] To a disinterested observer, that would seem to be an exaggeration. Just as some charters do better and some do worse, when public charter schools end up being in the top 10 percent of English and math scores of all your high schools in a state, then they are doing something right for the high-needs black and Hispanic student body that they primarily serve in some states. This model should not be limited but rather encouraged to expand for the good of our children.

The actual NEA Policy Statement on Charter Schools adopted by seven thousand delegates to their 2017 annual meeting is quite straightforward in its systematic design to thwart more school choice. It is an iron fist in a cotton glove. The NEA policy statement claims that the public charter schools "are not subject to the same basic safeguards and standards that apply to public schools, [which] threatens our students and our public education system." That is a high charge to level against public charter schools that have administrators, teachers, teacher aids, and other staff all working for the betterment of the students that come through their doors just like the neighborhood public school around the corner or even in the same building if the two are colocated in the same school. There is no objective proof that the teachers in one school care more or less than the teachers in another school. There is no objective proof that the

---

[100] Celeste Busser, "NEA Adopts Charter School Policy Statement," July 4, 2017, NEA press release.

[101] Id., (emphasis added).

[102] Id.

administrators in a neighborhood public school care more than the administrators in a public charter school. The threat, as the NEA sees it, is that as more students go to a public charter school, there will be fewer in the neighborhood school, so there will not be as many teachers in the neighborhood public school. This is not a decision to be made by the NEA or the local board of education. It is a decision to be made solely by the parents and guardians of the children who should be given more choices of where to send their children than those schools under the NEA and AFT umbrella.

The NEA thinks otherwise and, in a strategic move, has set forth policies in its 2017 statement that all but assure no more new public charter schools. "[C]harter schools be authorized only if they meet the substantive standards set forth in (a) below, and are authorized and held accountable through a democratically controlled procedure as detailed in (b) below." Before getting to the limiting criteria, the only reason that a parent or guardian of a black, Hispanic, Asian, or white child would consider sending their children to a public charter school is because the locally based traditional public school is controlled by a democratically elected political machine that is looking out for itself and not necessarily the children. If the democratically elected machine is broken, as evidenced by a school seen as failing by some parents and guardians, why would one think that this broken democratically elected machine would voluntarily relinquish control of a local resource to a public charter school that does not owe its allegiance to the local machine?

There is a reason that some state statutes, like Connecticut, allow the state Board of Education to review and approve of public charter applications. While the state Board of Education may also be beholden to a political machine, perhaps it is not as strongly limited as a local board of education, and in that instance, the state board of education may be willing to go against the local machine and authorize greater school choice. There is the image of Governor Andrew Cuomo, who used to be a strong proponent of public charter schools in Albany, bucking pressure from within his Democratic Party to give verbal support to the black, Hispanic, Asian, and white families that would trek to Albany to demonstrate for more public charter schools versus the more recent Mayor Bill de Blasio, who nonchalantly walks past black, Hispanic, Asian, and white students demonstrating for public charter schools at city hall without so much as stopping to commend them, because Mayor de Blasio is no friend of public charter schools in New York City.

Thus, the NEA designed its 2017 requirements so that the benefits of public charters to experiment or run more basic schools would be handicapped with the same rules and regulations of a neighborhood public school. And the simultaneous requirement that the proposed charter school proof show that they would not disrupt existing public neighborhood schools is akin to an environmental impact statement for construction or development projects. The proponents of a project submit an environmental impact statement that says, with remedial measures, there would be no adverse environmental impact from the proposed development. Opponents, however, can cry foul and bring a lawsuit to challenge the environment impact statement, meaning further delay in building the project. Time is money, and time delays will defeat countless construction projects. By the same token, the requirement to show that a new or expanded public charter school would not negatively impact the existing local public school is like an environmental impact statement and would likewise defeat many efforts to create or move students to a public charter school. Public charter schools do not have stacks of money behind them. Instead, public charter schools sometimes look to federal grants to get the seed money to start a public charter school. But if the state and/or local approvals for the public charter school doesn't come, then there is nothing to open and give a grant to. The NEA wants (1) open meetings; (2) prohibitions against for-profit operation or profiteering as enforced by conflict of interests, financial disclosure, and auditing requirements; (3) the same civil rights and protections for students with disabilities, employment, health, labor, safety, staff qualification, and certification as other public schools. If the local school has a collective bargaining agreement, which means it is unionized, then the new charter school has to be unionized.[103] The policy recommendations also said:

> The public charter school may be authorized or expanded only after a district has assessed the impact of the proposed charter school on local public school resources, programs and services, including the district's operating and capital expenses, appropriate facility availability, the likelihood that the charter will prompt cutbacks or closures in local public schools, and consideration of whether other improvements in either educational program or school management (ranging from reduced class sizes to community or magnet schools) would better serve the districts needs.[104]

A fair reading of these requirements shows that there is no way a charter would not impact the local public school. If a local public school district is asked whether they would like to try to experiment with a magnet school, which they control, or a public charter school, which they would not control, it is obvious that they would opt for the magnet school ten out of ten times. This is a formula for a public charter school applicant to fail by design.

That is just the beginning of the NEA charter school requirements.

> The district must also consider the impact of the [public] charter on the racial, ethnic and socio-economic composition of schools and neighborhoods and on equitable access to quality services for all district students, including stu-

---

[103] "NEA Policy Statement on Charter Schools," adopted by the 2017 Representative Assembly, July 4, 2017, ra.nea.org, accessed October 6, 2020.
[104] Id.

dents with special needs and English language
learners. The impact analysis must be independent, developed with community input, and be
written and publicly available.[105]

And to think that it is not enough for the parents and guardians to decide for their children for a different way than the existing neighborhood school that they believe will fail their child. The
experts will decide for you. In these days of strained fiscal budgets,
it is unlikely that a cornucopia of funds will be made available to
either the neighborhood public school or the public charter school.
If money can be found for a local neighborhood school and can also
be found for local children going to a public charter school, these
new monies could be used for both. But here again with an impact
analysis is a second form of obstruction of school choice, for the
impact analysis can be contested in court just like an environmental
impact statement.

The NEA was only getting started. They are very good at what
they do. Then came part b of their policy statement:

Public charters schools should only be authorized by the same
local democratically accountable entity that oversees all district
schools such as a locally elected school board, or if there is no school
board, a community-based charter authorizer accountable to the
local community.[106]

The rest of the justification reiterates in many different ways
that the local political machine shall maintain control. There cannot be a "diffuse authorization system…with differing partial views
of the students seen by the district." Ironic that they should reference "differing partial views of the students" as being in error when
the person or persons with the best full view of the students are
their parents and guardians! To make sure that the state cannot get
involved, the NEA would limit the state's role in approving public
charter schools "to ensuring that local school districts only authorize

---

[105] Id.
[106] Id.

charters that meet the criteria in [sections a and b]." In other words, a governor like New York's Andrew Cuomo, who used to promote public charter schools, would be powerless to stop a mayor like New York City's Bill de Blasio and his political allies from crushing the public charter schools in New York City that outperform or perform as well as their neighborhood public schools, regardless of the black, Hispanic, Asian, and white voices pleading on the steps of city hall for these students to be able to attend these schools. "States should entertain appeals from approvals or denials of charters only on the *narrow grounds* that the *local process* for approving a charter was not properly followed or that the approval or denial of a charter was arbitrary or illegal. (emphasis added)"

So there you have it. No more expansion or new public charter schools in jurisdictions with high-needs black and Hispanic students that have been controlled by the same political party for the past fifty years. And who is the opponent of school choice? And who is the proponent of school choice?

Even if one were to grant credibility to the NEA's huge boner that "studies document that charters, on average, do no better than public schools in terms of student learning, growth or development,"[107] it is for the people to decide and not the state. The state is there to serve the citizen. The citizen is the sovereign. When the parent or guardian decides that they would like to send their children to the public charter school that is "no better than [the local] public school," to use the words of the NEA, then that is what the citizen should be allowed to do! But the NEA is dead wrong on the performance of high-achieving public charter schools. The high-achieving public charter schools should be expanded and duplicated. Their funding should be increased to at least approach what is spent on comparable public schools. Just as it has been shown that colocated public charters and conventional public schools in the same building or neighborhood help each other's test scores, so, too, can an existing public school allow a public charter school to grow within the same building. This will be expanded upon later in this book, but briefly, if

---

[107] Id.

10 percent of the parents and guardians want a public charter school, then let it begin in the school where the kids are already. The physical building is already there. The transportation network is already there. The school nurse is already there. The sports fields are already there. The children already live in the neighborhood.

Lest one think the policy proposals of the NEA in 2017 ended the matter, the NEA was not through. It followed up with a scathing report in 2019: "State Charter Statutes: NEA Report Cards." The NEA posited whether it was possible that public charter school laws could pass an exam given by the NEA. Not surprisingly, public charter school statutes could not pass the NEA test! Grades were given by the NEA using the 2017 NEA-proposed policies as the standards by which to judge the state statutes.[108] NEA Senior Media Analyst Richard Allen Smith wrote in 2019 that for public charter laws to earn full points, the statutes for public charter schools must be "genuinely public, transparent and accountable, governed by local school boards, and high quality."[109] [110] In other words, the state statutes had to be written in a way to put public charter schools out of business and eliminate school choice for high-needs black and Hispanic students. The only choice that the NEA standards would allow would be within the public education monopoly allied with the NEA and AFT. The school-to-prison pipeline must retain as many students as it can, otherwise the NEA and AFT will have fewer adult dues payers. We should not have to decide between the adults and our children. But if that choice is forced upon us, then we choose our children. A statutory scheme that leaves it to local school boards to voluntarily relinquish their students to a competing education model necessarily means that the students will not be released, and the students that need school choice the most will have it least.

How did the fifty states, Puerto Rico, and the District of Columbia do on the NEA exam? They failed miserably! "NEA...

---

[108] Richard Allen Smith, "Report: State charter school laws lack proper oversight," nea.org, May 9, 2019, accessed October 6, 2020.

[109] Id.

[110] "Richard Allen Smith," senior media strategist, www.linkedin.com, accessed October 7, 2020.

found that charter school statutes in nearly every state failed to meet basic standards for public oversight, accountability, transparency, local school board governance, and high quality education."[111]

Forty states received an F. Four states received a mediocre score of a D to a C-. Maryland did best with a B-, and six states don't even have legislation for public charter schools. Perhaps those six get an A for not even allowing public charter schools. With forty-four states out of fifty plus the District of Columbia and Puerto Rico getting a C- or worse, it would appear that plenty of Democrat-controlled, Republican-controlled, and bipartisan-controlled states failed the NEA test. Can it be that forty-four states are so out to lunch, whether Democrat or Republican, or is it that the NEA has an extreme agenda that will injure the chances for our children who may need it most?

Isn't the most important metric that a school gives high-quality education? Why would we care about the rest if a school model is giving high-quality education to all of its students—black, white, Hispanic, Asian, English-as-a-second language, and special-needs students? Surely we don't want our schools as cauldrons of corruption, nepotism, and be self-serving. But it would be hard to deliver high-quality education if a school were any of the negative things that Mr. Allen wrote about. To deliver high-quality education, a school has to be run with a dedication and commitment to our children. There was a slander made against General Ulysses S. Grant during the Civil War that he enjoyed liquor too much. Lore has it that during the North's campaign against the Confederacy, President Lincoln remarked in the nature of "If it was a fact that Grant enjoyed liquor too much then what brand of liquor does he drink, because I want to send him a case [since he was winning against the Confederacy]."

Upon review, the NEA Policy Statement on Charter Schools in 2017 is without peer in its potential to first curtail and then to slowly wipe away the existing charters. But that is the aim of the NEA to eliminate school choice for black, Hispanic, white, and Asian children outside of the school-to-prison pipeline. If the NEA

---

[111] Richard Allen Smith, "State charter school laws lack proper oversight."

had their druthers, there would not be any public charters and certainly not any public vouchers for high-needs black, white, Hispanic,
Asian, and other children to attend schools outside of the public
school monopoly run by the NEA and AFT. The requirement of the
NEA policy statement that "[p]ublic charter schools should only be
authorized by the same local, democratically accountable entity that
oversees all district schools such as a locally elected school board" is
genius of a malignant kind when the light of school choice is shown
upon it. That is not a level playing field. But it is not supposed to be
a level playing field.

Consider who the cheerleaders are for the local public school
board and the local neighborhood schools. It could be you and me.
We may have gone to the local schools, and we are still in the same
area. Friends are made in school. Good and bad experiences happen
in school, but we tend to remember the good and put the not so
good in a different category. There are some really good teachers,
academically but also personally. There may have been sports teams
that the citizen was on and played hard for such as the Gators or
Bulldogs or Capitals or Crimson, or whatever the sports figure was
for the school. Teammates worked together so that their school won
versus the other rival school. Bake sales were held to raise money for
uniforms or a travel budget. There were school dances and rallies.
Maybe there was a haunted maze for Halloween. And were there
some nice school parties or dances that the alumni remember?

Then you have our teachers, who are placed on a pedestal as a
general matter because of the awesome responsibility they undertake
to teach our students. These teachers could do other things, but they
are willing to take on the multiple tasks of teacher, mentor, and guide
for our young people as they grow up. Some teachers even reach into
their own pockets to buy supplies for their classroom to make up
for what budget shortfalls or simple incompetence fails to give the
teacher to do their job. From specific teacher to specific teacher, we
focus more on the good that they do than if they fail our students.
These teachers sometimes live in the same community as the school
in which they teach. The administrators such as principal, assistant
principal, guidance counselors, janitors, cooks, teacher aides, and

other people critical to the functioning of a school may also live in the area.

The politics of the local school district also comes into play. There are politicians who serve as mayors and first select people, and they might be of the same party that controls the local board of education. Chances are that the board of education for a failing school has probably been controlled by the same political party for decades. And if there is no other political power within the local community that could displace the ruling party, what motivation does the local political party have of reforming itself or overturning the applecart? There is little motivation. Furthermore, the people who have moved up in the school system as administrators may well have taught in the local schools and/or may have friends and allies within the local dominant political party.

Don't forget about the local Parent Teachers Association or PTA! Those parents of students in the local school system are doing what they can do to help the education of the community's children. It might be as chaperones on a school trip. Maybe it is to assist with an after-school program. Or there are the basic bake sales and car washes held to raise money so that teaching supplies or computer equipment can be purchased for the local school to help with what is or is not already there. Parents will like their local teachers. Local PTAs will support their schools. Why would a local PTA support legislation or new public charters that could take students and ultimately funding away from their local public school, even if that school has been consistently underperforming for its students? That would be a stretch to hope that the local PTA, the local teachers, the local administrators, and the local politicians would push hard for school choice, which encompasses public charter schools and vouchers. To hope to pass a new public charter school in the face of all these natural allies for the local public school would almost be a suicide mission. Why should the local community gut the local school of students, funding, and by extension, teachers by supporting an alternative public school for local children? That is a stretch, and the NEA knows that.

If the public charter school choice has already been provided by the state authorities, then a parent or guardian can avail themselves of that choice without having to run the gauntlet of supporting an unpopular solution to the local school board. Which local school board that you know wants to be put out of business? None. They will fight their darnedest to stay in business and therefore to stay relevant. By giving the parents and guardians from high-needs families a choice, you are not forcing these parents and guardians of running the gauntlet at a public meeting and speaking out publicly against the local students, local teachers, and local administrators, and saying some not so nice things about the teachers there. People remember, and they live in your community.

Which comes back to the first question posed by the NEA's anti-charter school policy statement. Why would any local school board support new charter schools or the expansion of existing public charter schools? They wouldn't. And that is the genius but also cynicism of the NEA policy statement. If the NEA's policy statements were adopted at the state level, then new public charter schools would cease to be authorized, and school choice would be dealt a blow. A charter school applicant who would try to get their charter school approved would have to convince the local school board that it is a good idea. The proponents of the new charter school would likely only be the potential organizers who have to put an application and budget together. Then there would be some vocal parents and guardians who would speak for school choice. But the number of charter proponents at a local level would be swamped by the existing alumni and alumnae, teachers, administrators, politicians, and the very influential local PTA, who would speak against the application and pronounce that the public charter had already failed before even opening its doors. That some public charters might win that fight is possible, but the effort to create new charters or expand existing charters at the expense of the local schools would be slim. That is why it is better to do it at the state level, where it is more likely to be framed as an expansion of school choice for high-needs children, and the state board of education people may not be as beholden to local interests to keep a failed school or two going *ad infinitum*. There may be a greater interest at the state level to see English, math, and other academic disciplines learned at a higher rate across the state. One would hope.

The NEA knows this, which is why they have written their policy statement to ensure domination and elimination of public charters. It is all about the number of members that the NEA has and the dues-paying ability of the members to fill the coffers of the NEA's political action committee and to fund more all-expense paid junkets to comfortable meetings and get more legislation to favor the NEA and AFT over the children they are supposed to be serving. What if a miracle happened and the NEA were unsuccessful at having the local political authority deny a new public charter school? The NEA has that covered too with their proposed policies. If the local democratically elected school board were to approve a charter, then if that "public school district has an existing collective bargaining agreement with its employees, the authorizer will ensure that the employees will be covered by a collective bargaining agreement." So there are only two good charter schools: (1) a dead one or (2) one that is covered by a collective bargaining agreement negotiated by representatives of the NEA or AFT. That seems to be a very limited view of what should be available to our children and young adults. Could it be that only a public charter school that has been unionized and is affiliated with the NEA or AFT is able to run a good public charter to the exclusion of all the public charter schools that outperform the local public school in our nation? It is hubris to propose that the only people who know how to run a public charter school are those with union pedigree. That appears to be too much of a black-and-white view of the world. Only if organized by the NEA or AFT can a public charter school be acceptable. This again underlines that the allegiance of the NEA and AFT is first and second to the teachers and the union, all of whom are adults, and that our children and young adults only come in third place after the adults have been satisfied.

Another way to look at the unfairness of the NEA proposal for a public charter school to be judged by their competitors down the street is what the prognosis is for inventions. In an economy, there are existing technologies and inventions that we use to live and work. We are comfortable with what we know and live with.

When a new invention comes in with a new way to do something, it may not be embraced right away, but it has the potential to displace existing products and technologies. When horse carriages were used, there were jobs and suppliers catering to horses—feeding horses, housing horses, and making horse carriages, covered and uncovered. Veterinarians cared for horses. Wood was supplied to make carriages. When automobiles and trucks started to be invented and powered by steam or the internal combustion motor, it threatened the trades and suppliers around horse-drawn carriages. The shift was not immediate in the West, but over decades, horses to move people and goods were put out of business except for recreational purposes or ranching, but they were altogether supplanted. This meant that people in the old horse and buggy industries had to shift to a new line of work or be out of work. On the other side of the coin, those who took to making cars and trucks, supplying the coal for steam engines or gasoline to run the internal combustion motors, found employment and opportunity. As the mass of the people chose the newer invention over the older way, the economy changes and progresses as a better way is found.

The invention of the light bulb did not sweep candles away overnight, but certainly over twenty to thirty years cities started to use light bulbs to light their streets, and people started to use light bulbs to light their homes and seize the night from darkness. Fewer candles were sold. All the people who made a living from making and selling candles and all the people making horse buggies or caring for the horses that pull those buggies had a natural interest to see that the existing technology continue. What happens if the suppliers and producers of an existing technology are asked whether a new invention should be tried that has the potential to put their type of technology or product out of business? Chances are that most of those stakeholders would vote no. There would be some agile or venturesome types that might vote yes, but not enough to wave out the old technology and wave in the new. As votes are usually carried by a majority of just over 50 percent, that is a high hurdle to get a technology to vote itself out of business. That is precisely what the NEA policy statement banks on. No way will a local democratically accountable entity that oversees all district schools like a school board vote to open schools that could siphon off half or all of their students. It's not going to happen.

Would public charter school opponents claim that they are doing this to help black, Hispanic, white, Asian and other students in the existing public schools from losing resources? Of course. That is their marketing. The only reason public charter schools are being pursued is that some local public schools are seen as failing the educational needs of our students in urban, suburban, and rural settings. If we are spending twice as much per student, after adjusting for inflation today as we were spending in 1960, is the education being provided twice as good or the same or worse than 1960 in terms of English language skills and math? If the performance is not twice as good, then the traditional model is not keeping up with its cost to the citizenry. If the math and English abilities of our young is at or near the levels it was in 1960, then something is woefully wrong. Are the young adults who get into college and universities arriving with the same math and English skills as in 1960, or are colleges and universities putting these students into remedial courses to get them up to the level of 1960?

This begs the question, Who has strengthened their presence in the public school system since 1960? And did it benefit adults more or students more?

Not to be outdone by the NEA, the AFT has also been playing a heavy hand against school choice primarily for black and Hispanic students. The AFT proudly published and boasted that they supported a national moratorium on new charter authorizations in line with the quixotic policy of the NAACP.[112] It appears that the head of the NAACP does not know what the body wants. The national AFT supported a cap on public charter school expansion in the Los Angeles Unified School District and California.[113] That is quite bold to support a moratorium across the country on new public charter schools! Whose interest is the AFT looking out for to know the con-

---

[112] "AFT Resolutions and Policy," July 2018–2020.
[113] Id.

ditions across the fifty states and what parents and guardians want? A moratorium would mean the voices of black, Hispanic, white, Asian, and non-English-speaking parents and guardians would not be heard. The parents and guardians who already have their children in public charter schools want to get siblings into the same schools. The parents and guardians of children on waitlists, would be told by the AFT to go to the end of the line and accept the status quo. Their voices don't count. Consider the performance of the Stamford Charter School for Excellence, which had only been in existence for less than five years when its third and fourth graders crushed English and math tests in Connecticut in 2018 to 2019. If one were to consider that some of the best K-12 schools in New York City are public charter schools with high-needs black, white, Hispanic, Asian and other children, it shocks to see the AFT promote a blanket moratorium of trying to mimic those successes in more public charter schools! That is a one-size-fits-all mentality.

For a union that says it is about high-quality education, the expectation is that the AFT would embrace public charter schools that deliver high-quality education and not see them as a threat to the existence of the AFT. It is like when Thomas Edison invented the light bulb. The Flat-Earth Society declared that "the candle industry was threatened today!" Think of the good that came from light bulbs at seizing back night for use to read and be productive versus the dim light of candles, not to mention the benefit of lighting streets. Public charters can work with AFT members and, both union-run schools and public charters can deliver quality education to our children.

Instead, public charters are struggling to teach the children in their care against the headwinds of running a school, plus the organized resistance of an entrenched bureaucracy that tilts toward the status quo. Has the status quo historically served black and Hispanic students?

Not only did the AFT want to put a moratorium on public charter schools, at best, they also were proud to reduce the testing of student progress in English and math. The AFT boasted of reducing testing in the Los Angeles school district by 50 percent. Perhaps testing has gotten out of hand and teachers felt they were teaching to the tests and not teaching for a life's education. That certainly can have merit, but do you boast that you have reduced testing by 50 percent?[114] That can be another method to reduce accountability of individual teachers. How do you promote and pay effective teachers more and train and counsel those who don't achieve adequate results? Isn't testing part of that metric?

With the arrival of the COVID-19 pandemic in March 2020, the routines of many schools were upended and ultimately closed for the spring school year. The fall school year opened with fits and starts, with much of the teaching happening online. There were hybrid programs where maybe a quarter of the students would come to the physical school on one day and then another quarter the next day. Then those at home would learn over the video feed from the teacher at school or some other online alternative. Yet the NEA had been pretty adamant about the value of online schooling for our children in the NEA Policy Statement on Charter Schools in July 2017: "[Fully virtual or online charter schools] should not be authorized as charter schools."[115] That is a pretty open and shut case for the NEA. "Fully virtual or online charter schools cannot, by their nature, provide students with a well-rounded, complete educational experience, including optimal kinesthetic, physical, social and emotional development."[116] In law school, they encouraged students not to say *always* and *never* because the law often has exceptions and life is messy. In retrospect, it is anticipated that the NEA would amend their blanket opposition to online charter schools. Even before the pandemic, it is not for the NEA to say that online schools should never be authorized. That, again, is up to the parents and guardians. It may be that the parents supplement the lessons of the school with their own homeschooling as well as values.

Would the Connecticut AFT consider any different view on public charters in view of some of the local successes in Connecticut? One would hope, but the same monolithic opposition to school

---

[114] "AFT State of the Union 2018–2019," p. 8.
[115] "NEA Policy Statement on Charter Schools," July 4, 2017.
[116] Id.

choice for high-needs children prevailed there also. In fact, in 2020, AFT Connecticut was even more clairvoyant on the value of school choice. On the Connecticut AFT website, they boasted that they can tell you "The Truth About Charter Schools!"[117] That is a pretty tall order to have discovered the truth. The Connecticut AFT opined that the public charter schools have not shared their innovations with conventional public schools.[118] That's interesting that the Connecticut AFT believes that there are innovations that are worth sharing. That means that some of the public charter school methods in Connecticut are in fact effective for teaching our students, from whatever background they may come. If public charters were "no better in results" as the national AFT maintains than our neighborhood schools, then why would the Connecticut AFT wish that the public charters share their innovations? Because those innovations work. That is the purpose of charters—to innovate and to teach.

The Connecticut AFT goes further to slander public charters to say that they increase racial and ethnic isolation and point to Achievement First's Bridgeport Academy at 98.7 percent minority and Achievement First's Hartford Academy at 99.5 percent minority, which is above the minority composition of Bridgeport schools at 91.45 percent and Hartford at 92.6 percent. The fact that minority parents and guardians are trying harder to take advantage of the school choice offered by public charters is evidence not of why the Connecticut AFT should oppose these schools for blacks, whites, Hispanics, Asians and others, but as a reason to open up more slots and to let these public charters have seats for the over six thousand children on waitlists to get in. The day that there are no children on these waitlists for public charter schools is the day on which the Connecticut AFT can raise their first question about their efficacy and place of public charters. Before then, the Connecticut AFT is out of place to object to the free choice of the parents and guardians from high-needs communities to send their children to public charters!

---

[117] "The Truth About Charter Schools," aftct.org, accessed October 5, 2020.
[118] Id.

Parents and guardians know what is best for their children, far better than the statists at the AFT and their brethren! Do not stand in the way of these parents and guardians.

Not satisfied to rely on a meritless claim that some public charters increase racial isolation, the Connecticut AFT libels public charters further by raising the canard that the public charters pull the "best of the best." It can be conceded that a public charter will most likely tell a parent or guardian that there are expectations of the parent and guardian as well as the student for the effort that must be undertaken at the school. That is nothing more than expectations. If you don't have expectations of a person, then that person will not try to meet those expectations. If there are no standards of conduct, then you will necessarily be disappointed in the conduct since no level has been specified. But if we go back to the canard that only the best of the best are selected, that might be plausible if there were an admissions process. Instead, the slots are filled by lottery. Lotteries are necessarily random. In 2020, Connecticut had about ten thousand public charter students and over six thousand on waitlists. The Connecticut AFT would have the public believe that those sixteen thousand young people are the best of the best. That is an absurdity. Could that even be statistically possible?

The Connecticut AFT also warns ominously that dark corporate money is behind funding these evil schools. What a terrible thing to give educational opportunities to these children. Their article maintained that in Michigan, four out of five charters were run by for-profit organizations. This book does not tout for-profit over nonprofit charter schools, as it is for the parents and guardians in each instance to make their own evaluation. If the charters are expanding in Michigan, then why should this "be deeply, deeply troubling for anyone thinking about their child's further education, or the future of this country"?[119] If more and more parents are voluntarily picking public charters over their neighborhood school, those parents and guardians are doing it precisely because they are "thinking about their child's further education [and] the future of this country." Dr. Miron has it wrong.

---

[119] Id., quoting Dr. Gary Miron.

The truth behind Connecticut AFT's vehement opposition to public charters comes out further on their website because they believe the money should not follow the child: "The financial impact of money 'following the child' to a charter school affects the remaining public school students." The Connecticut AFT estimated that in 2011 to 2012, town and regional school districts across Connecticut spent on average per student of $14,122. Thus, posited the Connecticut AFT, what if three students left and took that funding with them? This would amount to more than the average starting salary of a beginning teacher of $39,259, which would not have included pension and health care benefits. Increasing class sizes whilst they have fewer students to teach, according to the Connecticut AFT, could lead to lower test scores at the neighborhood school, that students were leaving already. "If test scores start to drop, there will be increasing dissatisfaction in the district—potentially causing more students to opt out of the public system in favor of charter schools. And that's how the downward spiral could signal the end of a school."[120]

The net beneficiaries in that scenario would seem to be the students as they have gravitated toward higher academic performance. That would be a public good. But this straw man runs counter to experience. When public charters are located in the same building as a neighborhood school or is within half a mile of a similar grade level neighborhood school, the performance by each has been shown to get better at each institution and not worse. That is the benefit of competition. The goal is not to put neighborhood schools out of business but to make them better and at the same time to give educational choice to children from these communities.

One of many problems with the hatchet job delivered by Connecticut AFT is that they were still stuck in a time warp of 2012. In 2020, their attack pieces seem to have been unchanged since 2012, although the same page was informing the public that their headquarters had closed in March 2020 due to the coronavirus. In addition, the Legislative/Political Action Committee meeting would be held on October 6, 2020. It was as if nothing had

---

[120] Id.

transpired in eight years. They still featured headline grabbing links to stories about "Charter School Corruption" and "How Charter Schools Fleece Taxpayers." The "Charter School Corruption" article reported on some charter schools that had to refund some monies in Ohio and the closure of a charter in California. The reader is invited to go to a website: charterschoolscandals.blogspot. And that is how it should be. If a public charter school is mismanaged and cannot run their affairs, they are either shut down early by the state or their three, four, or five-year charter is not renewed. But what happens to an itinerantly failing neighborhood public school? Is that closed? Unlikely. If there is a revolving door of principals, does that change the trajectory of the school? If financial improprieties are discovered at a local public school, what is typically done? Rarely, if ever, is a local public school closed as the political interests and inertia are so great it can plod along with promises from the mayor and board of education that they are going to shake things up and fix the problems. And if the problems don't get fixed, what is the alternative for children from high-needs communities? The money is not there by definition. They cannot go off to another school unless the state is enlightened enough to offer vouchers to assist in tuition payment for a private school or public charter school choice. But if the opponents of school choice are successful, they would maintain a moratorium on new or expanded charter schools and continue to oppose vouchers that could be used for a local Catholic school, for instance, a la Supreme Court Justice Sonia Sotomayor, originally from public housing in New York City.

If a public charter is failing or rife with financial improprieties, it doesn't get its limited charter renewed. If a neighborhood public school is failing or rife with financial improprieties, it can keep going for decades. Why must the children suffer? Another old article featured by the Connecticut AFT was in *The New Republic*: "How Charter Schools Fleece Taxpayers."[121] That article focuses primarily on Arizona charter schools and that some had contracted with family

---

[121] Timothy Noah, "How Charter Schools Fleece Taxpayers," *The New Republic*, November 20, 2012.

members or board members to provide services to the schools. Other references were to conflicts of interest in real estate deals. The article finished with the observation that in addition to offering an opportunity prior to 2012 for self-enrichment, "some public-private experiments in K-12 education are free of any tedious public obligation to demonstrate that anybody on the premises is learning anything at all." Hmmm? Not learning anything at all? I wonder how long the parents and guardians of students of such charters, where children are "not learning anything at all," would leave their children at such institutions? The difference between having public charter schools and vouchers is that the parents and guardians have a choice, whereas in the latter approved model of the AFT and NEA, they have no choice. And it is more likely that the school-to-prison pipeline flows from failing public neighborhood schools than public charter schools or private schools like Catholic day schools.

Why do charters excel in some instances to be leagues above their neighborhood schools with similar student bodies? And how can the public charters and conventional schools collaborate on curriculum for the benefit of our students? By cooperating and adopting more rigorous academic standards.

Chapter 18

What Kind of Curriculum Could Our K-12 Neighborhood Schools or Public Charter Schools Aim For?

WHAT CURRICULUM SHOULD a neighborhood public school or a public charter school teach? The goal of our K-12 schools is not just to get somebody ready to continue to college or to learn a trade. Rather, it is to form a well-rounded citizen that is able to realize their potential in life and to participate and support our democratic system of government, namely the Rule of Law where the citizen is sovereign and not some dictator. That means a curriculum that gives the student the tools of citizenship to be exposed to different ideas and to be able to evaluate them on their own. The Declaration of Independence in 1776 and the drafting of our Constitution in 1787 were the most significant advancements in the political history of mankind ever. For the first time, the government would be of the people and by the people and not by some king, queen, ruler, dictator, khan, sultan, or tribal leader based on family lines or sheer brawn. The president would be the first servant of the people. The Rule of Law is on the other side of the Rule of Man, which has been the condition of man since men and women came to be created on this earth.

English and math are critical to developing the mind of young people, and it is a convenient metric to measure the effectiveness of a school in teaching its students. If a citizen lacks the ability to read the written word and to speak the language, it makes working and participating in society more difficult. Decent English and math abilities can help a person advance in their work and to earn a better living and thereby try to achieve their version of the American dream easier.

One can look to W. E. B. DuBois and his recommendation of the curriculum at Atlanta University in 1903. Who was W. E. B. DuBois? William Edward Burghardt DuBois was born in 1868 in Great Barrington, Massachusetts, only a few years after the end of the Civil War. Mr. DuBois's maternal great-great-grandfather had been a slave from West Africa. W. E. B. DuBois was raised in Great Barrington. He was a minority in a white community and attended the local public school and played with his white schoolmates.[122] The teachers recognized that he was a gifted student. After he graduated from Searles High School, the First Congregational Church of Great Barrington raised money for his tuition to Fisk University, a historically black college in Nashville, Tennessee.[123] There he was exposed to Southern racism, Jim Crow laws, and lynching. He graduated in 1888. Thereafter, he attended Harvard University and graduated *cum laude* with a degree in history in 1890. With a fellowship from the John F. Slater Fund for the Education of Freedmen, he went and studied in Berlin, Germany. There he studied under the tutelage of prominent social scientists. After studying in Berlin, he returned to the United States and finished his graduate studies and was the first African American to earn a PhD from Harvard University. He was instrumental in the founding of the National Association for the Advancement of Colored People (NAACP) in 1909 and edited its magazine, *The Crisis*. Mr. DuBois saw the university as "a human invention for the transmission of knowledge and culture from generation to generation, through the training of quick minds and pure hearts, for this work no other human invention will suffice, not even trade and industrial schools."[124] While he did not say that he would

---

[122] "W. E. B. DuBois," en.wikipedia.org, accessed, October 13, 2020.

[123] Id.

[124] W. E. B. DuBois, *The Talented Tenth*, Writings (Penguin Books USA Inc., 1986), p. 847.

argue about what should be taught or how it should be taught, he did hold up the curriculum of Atlanta University as an example of a quality curriculum:

> One-fourth of this time is given to Latin and Greek; one-fifth to English and modern languages; one-sixth to history and social science; one-seventh, to natural science; one-eighth, to mathematics and one eighth to philosophy and pedagogy.[125]

The reference to a modern language would be something like French, Spanish, German, Italian, or Chinese. Social science was more narrowly focused on something that used to be called social studies. Today, it includes many subjects ranging from sociology, anthropology, economics, political science, psychology, and others. A natural science is related to the science of the earth and the world around us, such as biology, chemistry, physics, astronomy, and earth science. These are sometimes referred to as hard sciences and are included in what are popularly referred to as STEM programs for science, technology, engineering, and math. Mathematics is pretty straightforward, even if *new math* has made it less so. Philosophy is not so easy to explain. *Webster's New World Dictionary* defined it as "1. originally, love of wisdom or knowledge. 2. a study of the processes governing thought and conduct; theory or investigation of the principles or laws that regulate the universe and underlie all knowledge and reality."[126] And then there is pedagogy, which is the art or science of teaching and teaching methods.

If a student were put through a curriculum based on these topics, he or she would be on the road to a good education and be an able citizen. Parents and guardians would like to have their children's minds filled with this knowledge and training.

---

[125] Id., p. 849.
[126] College Edition, The World Publishing Company, Cleveland, 1964, p. 1099.

What is lacking for some in this traditional curriculum would be political correctness, which is less about education and more about indoctrination in the political orthodoxy of the state. This has less to do about educating a strong citizen and more about teaching intolerance, as the more politically correct a person is, the more intolerant that person is. We should avoid teaching the intolerance of political correctness.

Chapter 19

What Kind of Curriculum Should Our K-12 Neighborhood Schools or Public Charter Schools Avoid?

S HOULD OUR SCHOOLS be a place for education, or should they also be a place for teaching political correctness? The reader would probably wholeheartedly agree that the political philosophy of Adolf Hitler and his National Socialist German Worker's Party should not be taught in our public schools![127] Adherents and proponents of the political positions and theories of Hitler's Socialist Workers' Party should probably not be teaching at our schools and universities. That would seem to be pretty straightforward and should not take much discussion. The murderous reign of the Nazi Party from 1933 to 1945 should and could be studied to help in lessons on how to avoid such an atrocity and to learn from the past and identify similar tactics and methods. The twelve-year reign of Hitler's one-thousand-year Reich was one of the most murderous of the last two centuries to the civilians who came under their jurisdiction before and during World War II, to include the Holocaust murder of six million Jews. Their political positions should not be proselytized in our schools, colleges, or universities. Why then would our nation

---

[127] The official name of Adolf Hitler's political party was National Socialist German Workers' Party, which made it a Socialist Workers' Party.

allow political positions espoused by Marxists and their fellow travelers to be proselytized at our schools, colleges, and universities is puzzling. These same Marxists, their fellow travelers, and useful idiots intimidate their fellow students, teachers, and administrators not through debate but intimidation, cancel cancer, and bullying.

What about Marxism and its offshoots of Leninism and Maoism? Should they be taught any differently than the National Socialism theories of Adolf Hitler? Marxism has been the deadliest political philosophy of the twentieth and twenty-first centuries to its own citizens. It has exceeded the murder count of National Socialism of Hitler by the forty million starved, tortured, and executed to death in Communist China since their seizure of power in 1949 and the twenty-two million citizens of the Union of Soviet Socialist Republics, the USSR, between their ousting of a liberal democratic government, the Provisional Government, in 1917 until the Soviet Union disappeared in 1991, to just take two examples. This does not even touch on *the Killing Fields* in Cambodia between 1974 and 1979 when millions were killed by the Marxists followers of Pol Pot and the Khmer Rouge. The hell of Communist North Korea and Communist Cuba continue to this day. Why should Marxism, Leninism, Maoism, and its theories, all of which propose a dictatorship of the proletariat which is no more than the Rule of Man as practiced for millennia of kings, queens, khans, dictators, tribal leaders, and strong men, versus the Rule of Law, where the citizen is sovereign, be taught in our schools as desirable? To hear that Marxism is a deadly philosophy can make a person's eyes glaze over with indifference. An American who did not immigrate to the United States from a country that has experienced the rule of fascists/communists/Marxists has little concept of the ways of Marxists. When millions of people are killed by starvation, execution, and torture, what could that mean? How is an American supposed to fathom such numbers?

After the killing of George Floyd in Minneapolis, Minnesota, in May 2020 by a white police officer holding his knee on George Floyd's neck for over eight minutes, months of protests followed in the United States and around the world. Most of the protests were peaceful, but in some jurisdictions, the protests became riots, and stores were looted, property destroyed, and cars burned. The appearance of people coming from outside the community would sometimes outnumber the people actually from the community. Washington, DC, found that 70 percent of the protestors arrested at one point were from outside of DC. When businesses were destroyed by looters and fires, local jobs were lost, local businesspeople and their life's work destroyed, and food deserts reappeared with the destruction of some stores such as Walmart. It will take some time to determine who these looters and rioters were and whether they shuttled around the United States to create maximum havoc regardless of its impact on the primarily African American neighborhoods and businesses that they attacked. How could it be that a white liberal could put on a *Black Lives Matter* T-shirt and go into a black neighborhood and set it on fire and then claim to be doing good work and seek accolades from others? Who will figure that one out?

The killing of Breonna Taylor in March 2020 in Louisville, Kentucky, by police officers executing a search warrant on her apartment was another example of excessive force, along with other black citizens who were killed in confrontations with the police. These and other events contributed to an outpouring of support for the black community across the country. Many politicians and business leaders scaled their soapboxes to say how they would make our society and economy better. And one of the rallying cries was "*black lives matter*." At an NAACP-sponsored event in Stamford, Connecticut, a major boulevard was closed in coordination with the city on a Saturday in July 2020 to paint a Black Lives Matter mural in the street. There were community leaders as well as state, local, and federal elected officials on hand to give speeches. In the midst of the program, a black man interrupted and started to warn the crowd that Black Lives Matter was a Marxist organization and was inspired by Marxists. Ultimately, he stopped his protesting, the speeches continued, and he discussed his concerns with some of the Stamford NAACP members. No speaker on that stage, including Congressman Jim Himes, had any sympathy for Marxists or Marxism. They were all there in solidarity with the black community and to show their support, and their words showed that. What would possess a black man to interrupt this solemn event to warn of Marxist influence? Conceivably, it would have been more controversial for a white man or woman to interrupt the solemnity of the ceremony but less so for a black man. That took guts. What did he know that we didn't know? There have been stories that some of the leaders of this leaderless movement had Marxist inclinations. The point here is not whether they did or did not, but why would a man of color take the time to interrupt a solemn event to warn of Marxist influence? Because Americans have little idea of what Marxism, Leninism, or Maoism entails. If Americans had an equal awareness of the lethality of Marxist dictatorships, they would be more tuned in to how Marxist theories are pressed on our students and now into general society.

> [For Marxists] to kill unarmed civilians in large numbers, often including women and children, is an act that invokes norms of battlefield combat. It is insufficient simply to designate as subhuman a category of individuals who are subject to surveillance and discrimination, as in China with its "class enemies" after the Land Reform movement of the 1950s.[128]

According to author Yang Su, collective killings in China during the Cultural Revolution took place in public. These public killings usually took place after a "struggle rally on a village square enumerat[ing] the Four Types' 'evil attempts' and pronounced the decision of the 'mass dictatorship.'"[129]

> On the morning of June 16, 1968, a landlord's wife and two of her sons were tortured and killed on the rally stage in Niancun Village in Cangwu County in Guangxi Province.[130]

---

[128] Yang Su, *Collective Killings in Rural China during the Cultural Revolution* (Cambridge University Press), 191.

[129] Id., p. 217.

[130] Id., p. 218.

Where a condemned man had snatched a gun from his escort [Quing's brigade] and escaped, he later shot a man.

> [The escaped man's] two adult brothers were killed quickly, whereas his mother and two younger brothers were saved for the revenge of Quing's brigade. In a rally on June 16, Quing's brother cut off the ears of the escaped man's mother and younger brothers and then stabbed them to death. The atrocities unfolded on stage in front of hundreds of villagers.[131]

> The killings were typically carried out using various farm implements.[132]

This is government policy to systematically kill their own citizens in front of the people to further terrorize the people and maintain control. Marxists do not stand for elections. Once they have seized power, there is rarely a free election thereafter. Mao Zedong and his Communist Party, who won the civil war in China in 1949, have never held a free election from then to this day.

What is ironic is that countless Americans have adopted Marxist inspired analysis to call themselves privileged and that they apologize for that. *Privileged* is just another Marxist construct. It is merely a different word for *bourgeois* or *petit bourgeois*. The word *privileged* can be interchanged with *bourgeois* or *petit bourgeois* and still come up with the same meaning. It would just be too obvious if Marxists, their fellow travelers, and useful idiots went around calling others bourgeois. But to someone who has immigrated to the United States from a country that has more Marxists, the similarity is clear. These Americans who are labeling themselves privileged have no idea why they are doing it and what the significance is. They are not aware of what Marxists do to people who they identify as bourgeois, petit

---

[131] Id.

[132] Id.

bourgeois, or capitalist! The Marxists, Leninists, and Maoists take away the property of the privileged. Some are imprisoned. Some are tortured. Some are starved, and many are executed. It all depends on the level of control that the Marxist have of a country and their need to terrorize the citizens to stay in power.

In Mao's China, they practice a form of primogeniture as had been practiced in Europe where the oldest son would inherit the estate of the father. The Chinese communists would ascribe the crimes of the father to his offspring. So if the father was deemed to be a rich landlord or rich farmer, then they could drag the son up on the stage during a struggle rally in front of the village, castigate him, denounce him for his lineage from a rich landlord, and then kill him in front of his neighbors by hand. In 1968, Huang Caijiao, the sixteen-year-old son of a former landlord, did not die from the initial attack with farm implements after a struggle rally. He tried to crawl away. "Huang was quickly recaptured and escorted the next day to the same riverbank. The militia forced his cousin, the son of poor peasants, to finish the job. A witness [said] that using a hoe, the cousin "was trembling for the whole time.""[133]

Or consider the fate of seven men and one woman. Six were common criminals, including the woman who had killed her husband, and two who were considered counter-revolutionaries. The latter two were from the Harbin Electric Meter Factory and had been found guilty of publishing a flyer referencing the Soviet Union, thereby promoting Soviet-style revisionism. After the sentence was announced in a public square, they had signs hung around their necks and were paraded around Harbin on flatbed trucks.[134] They were driven to the outskirts of the city and followed by the public, made to kneel in a line, and shot in the back in the plain view of the crowd that had gathered to watch the execution.[135]

It was Chinese government policy to kill their own citizens by gun, knife, or farm implements on a public stage in order to indoc-

---

[133] Id., p. 218, quoting Cangwu Party Ratification Office, *The Causes for the Case that Killed Seven Family Members,* July 31, 1987.

[134] Li Zhensheng, *Red-Color News* Soldier, p.193.

[135] Id., ps.193–199,

trinate and intimidate her own citizens. Lest one think that the need to terrorize their own citizens was limited to the Communist Party of China, it was not. It is a universal trait of Marxist governments. Vladimir Ilyich Lenin pioneered the modern police state in the Soviet Union that he helped found in 1917 by seizing power from the liberal democratic Provisional Government. Aleksandr Solzhenitsyn, a one-time inmate of the Soviet prison system, documented the regularity of the seizing and imprisonment of the Soviet Union's own citizens in his three-volume *Gulag Archipelago*. Lenin, after all, coined the term *concentration camp* early in the establishment of the first Marxist dictatorship. In the eyes of the Leninists, a percentage of the population had to be seized in the dark hours of the morning and whisked off to the Gulag. Scurvy, lack of food, torture, and the like finished off many.

> But all that was too little, insufficiently strict, and the number of prisoners wasn't being sufficiently reduced. And so the "Garanin Shootings" began, which were outright murders. Sometimes to the roar of tractors, sometimes without... At Zolotisty they used to summon a brigade from the mine face in broad daylight and shoot the members down one after another. (And this was not a substitute for night executions; they took place too.)[136]

This, too, was government policy in Soviet Russia to systematically execute their own citizens. The use of trucks to shield the sound of executions duplicates the same technique used by Lenin's executioners to idle a truck outside the Ipitiev House in 1918 where they shot Russian czar Nicholas, his wife, their cook, physician, and other adults and then used bayonets, rifle butts, and handguns to personally murder the czar's four daughters and his hemophiliac son, otherwise the executions were making "too much noise" outside.

---

[136] *Gulag Archipelago* vol. 2, p. 128–129.

Soviet dictator Joseph Stalin later boasted that one death was a tragedy, but one million deaths was merely a statistic! This is the manner in which the communists kill their own civilians. How ignorant are we American citizens of the methods and theories of the Marxists!

Would that my fellow citizens were aware that when they parade around and flaunt their wokeness and declare themselves privileged that they are merely marking themselves for delegitimization as human beings, whereby what they say and think is not considered, and then later for elimination in the event Marxists ever gained power.

It is in this same line of delegitimating our fellow citizens that the politically correct work. It is not an accident. Cancel cancer is not an accident. It is a method. The idea behind political correctness is that there are specific political positions that one must take, otherwise the person or child will be castigated, reprimanded, or ignored by their teacher or school. For adults, there is a requirement to believe and support specific positions on the economy, health care, the environment, abortion, the role of religion, and social justice. The failure to adopt an approved position can subject that person to vilification and even something called cancellation. Cancelation is where the person is fired; their written materials are removed from circulation at colleges, universities, and even by publishers themselves; and the person is generally castigated. The person is held to be less than human by these promotors of cancel cancer. Others have called it cancel culture, but a culture is alive, and cancel cancer is vigorous on the outside in stamping out opposing viewpoints and dead on the inside as the pursuit of knowledge and the truth is stopped. Humility, compassion, forgiveness, and redemption have no room in cancel cancer.

In fact, the more politically correct a person is, the more intolerant they are. This is verified by the simple question asked of any woman or man in the street: "Do you agree that the more politically correct a person is, the more intolerant they are?" And the almost universal answer is yes. The more politically correct you are, the more intolerant you are. Any poll that asks that question without qualification will come to the same result. This should not come as a surprise as the most intolerant people are Marxists and their fellow travelers. These are the forces on college campuses that have terrorized their fellow students, professors, and administrators. Now they are sending their intolerance into the general economy and society. Marxists are not interested in argument or debate but rather power.

Why bring this up? Because it is relevant to what type of curriculum should not be taught at our schools. And that is the intolerance of political correctness. And that is teaching the orthodoxy of the state. Our children and young people should be taught in academics and have their minds trained to think. They should not have the theories of the most intolerant ideologies of the twentieth and twenty-first centuries taught to them, whether our children are in the local neighborhood public school or public charter school. If the public is paying, and the public is paying, then Marxism, Leninism, Maoism, and National Socialism should not be taught other than in a history class to examine the horror of the Rule of Man versus the Rule of Law. A good education and the ability to analyze different ideas is important to staying out of the school-to-prison pipeline.

Chapter 20

Proposed Legislation to Increase School Choice for all Students

A S A FREE society, education is imperative to our survival. It was an educated citizenry in the New England of 1776 that put New England leagues ahead of the old civilizations of Europe and Asia. Universal education is important. Methods that we can do to educate our citizens in knowledge and the ability to think are important to the foundation of our society. Since public charter schools and vouchers help spread quality education more evenly through society, then they should be pursued even if it steps on the toes of the entrenched opposition of the NEA and AFT and their statist allies.

How could the educational prospects not just of high-needs black, Hispanic, white, Asian and other students be improved? By making it easier to invite public charter schools into our local schools. One should, for a moment, suspend the opposition by local administrators and board of educations to a hybrid form of education just because it is "more work." The "more work" is of an accounting nature. Thankfully, to immigration, our population in the United States is still growing. There are certain communities that may be seeing an influx of residents due to their job opportunities, housing affordability, cost of living, or scenic amenities, but generally speaking, populations are not growing by leaps and bounds.

We have the education physical plant that we need. School buildings will be replaced from time to time. But there is a local board of education, and there are bus routes to get students to school. Since the data shows that the colocation of a public charter school in the same building as a traditional local school increases the scores of both through competition, it is perfectly acceptable to have charters and traditional local schools in the same buildings. The infrastructure is already there. The sports teams are all there. Children on the traditional union-run side and the public charter side would eat lunch at the same time. They would have gym together. They would play on the same sports teams together. They would join the same afterschool programs. The difference is that their academic classes would be taught under two regimens in the same building.

An easy example is my high school, Greenwich High School, in Greenwich, Connecticut. I can already hear the opponents of school choice, the AFT, NEA, and the local PTA, get up and holler: "We don't need public charter schools here!" Greenwich is an affluent town with a diverse population and a higher percentage of English-as-a-second-language student body than most. The unique feature at Greenwich High School is that they have five different houses. It used to be four houses when I graduated in 1978: Clark, Bella, Folsom, and Sheldon. We had a graduating class of about 950, and the high school encompassed tenth through twelfth grade. Now the high school has grades nine through twelve. They have also shoehorned a fifth house into the school, Cantor. Each house has its own principal and clerical staff. Nonetheless, the students from all houses travel to different houses, the science wing and art wing, to take their classes. If one-fifth of the parents and guardians of the high school opted to put their children in a public charter school at the high school, then one of the houses would be switched to a charter school. The students would take their academics at that house. They could take courses in other houses to fulfill their requirements.

Who would sign up, you ask? If a charter school offered the curriculum of Atlanta University as represented by W. E. B. DuBois, they would be swamped by parents and guardians seeking a traditional curriculum of Latin, Greek, English, French, Spanish, German, Italian,

Chinese, mathematics, philosophy, pedagogy, sociology, anthropology, economics, political science, psychology, biology, chemistry, physics, astronomy, and earth science. These young people will be educated and trained to think, the best defense for our democracy.

And no political correctness or orthodoxy of the state would be taught. Allow the parents and guardians to cover those subjects in intolerance and statism on their own time, if they so chose. These young people will be educated and trained to think.

It would not matter whether a school already had some different physical spaces, like Greenwich High School. All that would matter would be the desire of the parents and guardians who know their children best. Legislators and governors would have to work out the details in their statutory language in their own state capitals to achieve the goals of the parents and guardians. A possible version of statutory language to empower the parents and guardians of our children is "The School Choice and Voice Education Act."

The School Choice and Voice Education Act would allow the parents and guardians of economic, high-needs students to make their voice heard, and if enough parents and guardians in a particular school exercise their voice, then a choice will become available to the high-needs children of black, Hispanic, white, Asian, and other parents and guardians. That particular school building can be turned in part or whole into a public charter school. Parents and guardians of children in the school could sign a commitment to place their child or children into a public charter at that particular school. The signed commitments would be filed with the Registrar of Voters. Once 10 percent of the student body was reached within six months, then a public charter school would be instituted in the same building as the existing public school where the children are. After the verified commitments hit 10 percent, that choice could not be reopened for the subsequent school year to protect parents and guardians from bullying by representatives of the traditional, public school monopoly and their allies against school choice, the NEA and AFT. There would be no waitlists. After the 10-percent threshold is hit for high-needs students, the parents and guardians of other high-needs students at the school may add their children to the list for three months after the initial six month period expired. This will give the public charter school organization time to expand their student roles and make the public charter school more viable.

Should 60 percent of the parents and guardians of the students at the school choose the public charter option, then the entire school would be shifted over to a public charter school at a rental rate for the buildings and grounds of $1 per year for the identical school buildings and grounds as the school had used and had access to when the first elective forms were filed. A public charter school would have one year to hire its administrative and teaching staffs and open the doors to a new future in education at that school building. The public charter may use the same name and records of the existing public school that it would be taking over for.

For election levels below 60 percent down to 10 percent, so much of the school body whose parents and guardians chose to have the school transfer to a public charter would be effectuated by shifting the students of the parents and guardians who had exercised their right to choose into the new charter school to be colocated in the same building with the remaining students of the traditional public school. There would be no waitlists or lotteries to torment the parents, guardians, and their children with the hopes of a better future blocked by the vested interests of the status quo to the detriment of our children. All children of parents and guardians who wanted to establish a public charter school within the existing public school would be accommodated at that school provided that the minimum threshold of 10 percent had been met.

Neither the AFT nor the NEA nor their marionettes may question the efficacy of public charter schools so long as any child is on a wait-list to get into a public charter school in that state. This is respect for the citizen as opposed to bowing to the power of self-dealing factions. Under the foregoing example where a minimal charter had been voted in at 10 percent, 10 percent of the children would be in the charter school. That would leave the existing local school with 90 percent. In the politics of factions, 90 percent would represent an interest nine times bigger than the charter school students. The 10 percent would need protection from the 90 percent. This 90 percent might try to suppress, oppress, and/or intimidate these newcomers out of self-interest. What protections could be designed to shield these incubators of education? How could the children be saved from the machinations of adults against children?

Based on the number of students in the public charter school and the colocated traditional public school, the students from the public charter might attend French or Spanish classes taught by teachers from the other side of the school. Would there be a perverse incentive to give the charter students a worse grade so that the numbers for the charter would look worse than for the conventional school? A possible solution is that the public charter school would have a truncated curriculum to teach only charter students; and art and physical education classes, for example, might be taught with the students from the other side of the school but only on a pass-fail basis.

Funding for charter schools is different in different states. In Connecticut, the state gives $11,250 per student to the charter, so that helps build a budget for the school. The local school board reimburses the public charter for special education needs on top of that. A public charter would know how many students they would need in order to set up inside a specific public school. Let the public charter school state the minimum number of students it needs under the circumstances to operate, as that will vary on a case-by-case basis. Connecticut is particularly parsimonious in funding public charter students as it reflects the domination of Connecticut by statists who have consistently fought against school choice for high-needs black, Hispanic, white, Asian, and other students. These statists have held the number of our children in public charter schools in Connecticut at around 2 percent of K–12 students in the state and those not lucky enough to get in are forced to put their dreams on hold on a waitlist of six to seven thousand children lest the puppet masters of the statists not get enough at the public trough. Let the School Choice and Voice Education Act be the future of education in Connecticut and the other forty-nine states to put the education of our children in the hands of their parents and guardians who have the best interest of our children at heart.

Chapter 21

Factions and our Children

T HE NEA AND AFT are factions promoting their own interests before our children and our democracy. This is not to be confused with individual teachers who put their students first. When only 20.5 percent of black third and fourth graders in the Stamford, Connecticut school system in 2018–2019 were testing at or above grade level in math and black third and fourth graders at the Stamford Charter School for Excellence (SCSE) were scoring at or above grade level at 91.7 percent in the same town, that is a stark difference. The Connecticut public schools across the entire state failed miserably at the same time for the 2018–2019 school year at 21.7 percent at or above grade level for black third and fourth graders in math.[137] How has faction enabled this unreported scandal?

In the debates that followed the drafting of the United States Constitution in 1787, the most significant political document in the history of mankind, James Madison defined faction in *Federalist Paper 10* as "a number of citizens whether amounting to a major-

---

[137] Stamford Charter School for Excellence, *Appendix A: 2018-19 Charter School Annual Report,* October 18, 2019, submitted to Connecticut Department of Education, p. 9.

ity or minority of the whole, who are united and actuated by some common impulse of passion, or of interest, adverse to the rights of other citizens, or to the permanent and aggregate interests of the community."[138]

Based on the machinations set forth above to limit school choice for high-needs black, Hispanic, white, Asian, and other students by the NEA and AFT, the NEA and AFT fit the definition of a faction in that the fiduciary duty of the NEA and AFT to their members and to themselves is "adverse to the rights of [our children and their parents and guardians and] to the permanent and aggregate interests of the community [for a well-educated citizenry!]" In some states, there may be better progress in offering school choice for high need students, but in a state like Connecticut, public charters have been suppressed at less than two percent of the K-12 public school population and vouchers aren't even a thing in Connecticut! Would that Connecticut had a dominant political class that cared more about the education of our children than about the NEA and AFT, their affiliates, and getting statists elected.

In *Federalist Paper No. 10*, Mr. Madison proposed two ways to eliminate faction. One was to destroy liberty so that there could be no combining of interests. That was obviously a cure worse than the illness. The other was to require all citizens to have the same opinions, passions, and interests. This too was impractical, for so long as people were human, they would be fallible and have different tastes and opinions. Madison continued in *Federalist No. 10* and observed that the pure democracy of majority rule was the worst solution as a common passion would seize the majority who would be the government themselves as the majority "and there is nothing to check the inducements to sacrifice the weaker party."[139] That is what has transpired in the power machinations between the NEA, AFT, and our children. Our children's education has been sacrificed to the interest of the adult teachers and the adults' unions.

---

[138] James Madison, *The Federalist Papers*, No. 10, p. 78.
[139] Id., p. 81.

How easily can you fire an ineffective teacher? How easily can you get a school to get K-6 in-person teaching back in session after all of the teachers have been vaccinated against the Covid-19 coronavirus? The answer should have been days in 2021, but instead, it was a wait-and-see whilst the AFT and NEA representatives calmly set forth more conditions that would have to be met before the education of our nation's children could recommence in person. But certainly, keep the biweekly checks coming even while children from high-needs communities fall further behind their peers who are not from high-needs communities.

In drafting our constitution, a republic was supposed to be the better cure for the curse of factions. A republic would have numerous theoretical advantages. There would be more numerous citizens, and it would be spread over a larger geographic area. This would make it harder to coordinate these far-flung interests. That was in 1787 and thereafter. Certainly, the telephone, mails, and the Internet have made coordination and communication much faster to the point of instantaneous. It is true that with our republican form of government of fifty states, the District of Columbia, and various possessions that each of these entities is potentially able to find their own way. The problem is a strong faction from one state or many states can contribute to making a strong faction in another state and so on. Today, we have a most muscular NEA and AFT. Urban lore has it that when a software billionaire wanted to help society with his philanthropy, he considered improving the educational outcomes in the United States. It has been alleged that he was warned away from education and toward medical care as medical care was more amenable and welcoming to improvement. And the software billionaire and his wife have done wonders worldwide and at home in the medical field for which America and the world must be grateful!

How can K-12 education be improved when this muscular faction stands in the way, which in the words of Madison, "execute their plans of oppression?"[140] Madison's confidence was that "[t]he influence of factions leaders may kindle a flame within their particular

---

[140] Id., p. 83.

States but will be unable to spread a general conflagration through the other States."[141] Here, however, Madison was overconfident as exhibited by the width and breadth of the AFT and NEA today and their ability to keep the public school monopoly intact and deny school choice to our poor! The answer is enough legislators, governors, mayors, councilpersons, board of education members, and voters to insist on school choice for the poor and not-so-poor!

How obvious and persistent are the machinations of our teacher unions? A recommendation by an affiliate of the AFT in Connecticut presents a useful example. A president of the Hartford Federation of Teachers presented an opinion piece to an online journal, the CTMirror, in March 2021, "How to Close Schooling Opportunity Gaps Created by the Pandemic."[142] The author distinguished between what was seen as an achievement gap in scores between city schools and suburban schools and preferred to refer to it as an "opportunity gap" which encompassed important factors such as physically being in the same classroom with your peers, "sports, after-school clubs, singing, drama, assemblies, field trips, hands on activities, group projects, art projects, bands, etc." The author did acknowledge chronic absenteeism from the Covid-19 pandemic. The Hartford Federation of Teachers surveyed their members for how to close these opportunity gaps. About 1,170 teachers were surveyed with about 70 percent responding.

- Ninety percent of the teachers felt that there was no positive impact of an extended day at Hartford Public Schools at seven hours versus the traditional six hour school day. This would indicate that the school day should be shortened by one hour. So less school will get better results? It was left unstated whether the members would recommend a reduction in pay for one hour less in the school day?
- Eighty-nine percent said that adding more days to the school year or having a year round calendar would be inef-

---

[141] Id., p. 84.
[142] Carol Gale, *CT Viewpoints*, March 4, 2021

fective to support the students. So more schooling would not help the students?

- Seventy percent liked the idea of enrichment programs. That would be more pay or employees to be members of their union.
- Eighty-two percent supported increased services for social emotional growth. There was no definition for what that meant, but increased services would probably call for more part-time or full-time employees.
- Eighty-two percent thought there should be art and music for all students. That is a laudable goal, and one wonders why music is not available to all students?
- Eighty-nine percent favored increased tutoring opportunities. That would seem to call for tutors to be brought in as new employees.
- Eighty-four percent favored less standardized testing. Fewer standardized tests would compromise accountability of school and individual teachers. How does the taxpayer know which schools and teachers are more effective than others? Less accountability would appear to favor the AFT.
- Smaller class sizes were supported by ninety-six percent of the teachers. To achieve smaller class sizes, one has to hire more teachers who would become members of their union.
- Summer school results were only judged as effective at 55 percent.

The bulk of the Harford Federation of Teachers recommendations to close the achievement gap involved shortening the seven-hour school day, militating against school year-round, lessening accountability through standardized testing, and an increase in employees for the school system so as to add more dues payers to the local union. More art and music would be valuable additions.

The recurring problem is that increased expenditures have not translated to improved academics for our children. Public charter schools operate on fewer public dollars and deliver better results per dollar spent. It is guaranteed that if these recommendations of the Hartford Federation of Teachers were adopted to close the "achievement gap," the teachers and the union would benefit whilst expanding school choice through public charters and vouchers is left unmentioned.

To close an achievement gap, what about public charter schools focused almost exclusively on academics at a lower cost per student? How about giving the parents and guardians of our children a choice outside of the public school monopoly? The test results of the Stamford public school system for black and Hispanic students in English and math in the twenties and thirties at or above grade level in 2018–2019 are the equivalent of an indictment to a grand jury for the failure of the Stamford school system to teach our children when compared to the seventies, eighties, and nineties percentage of black and Hispanic third and fourth graders testing at or above grade level in math and English at the Stamford Charter School for Excellence! The entire state of Connecticut had equally miserable scores of 33.2, 21.7, 34.1, and 25.3 percent at or above grade level in math and English for black and Hispanic students. This is what you get with monopolies: overpriced and poor services, despite the valiant efforts of countless teachers and administrators within the public school monopoly. But we cower before the AFT and NEA factions. "Truth to power," "good trouble," and "wokeness" all ring hollow before the public school monopoly!

There seems to be an assumption that black and Hispanic students are expected to do worse in math and English; and therefore, few are alarmed at the uniform failure of the Connecticut and Stamford public school systems to change and embrace school choice. Public charter schools have shown that black, Hispanic, white, Asian, and other high-needs students can be top performers. Our expectations must change as well as the resistance to school choice.

Are there any consequences for the system-wide failure to teach and get the scores up for high needs black, white, Hispanic, Asian, and other students? Apparently, not in Connecticut. The system just goes along as if it is okay to assume that the Connecticut public-school system will continue to fail its black and Hispanic students. The public school monopoly that has run the public schools in Connecticut for decades just happily rolls on with its hand out for more money and saying that if they just had a few more dollars and a few more employees, then everything would be better. Fool me once, shame on you. Fool me twice, shame on me.

The Connecticut Commissioner of Education, Miguel Cardona, had been appointed by Governor Ned Lamont in August 2019. Commissioner Cardona was an affable and able man. He was not responsible for the failure of Connecticut's entire public-school system to teach black and Hispanic students with greater efficacy. It was not of Commissioner Cardona's making, although he was developed and elevated within that same monopoly. His appointment to Commissioner in 2019 would likely have made him a trusted steward of the status quo.

In 2021, there were more than one new proposed public charter schools approved by the Connecticut State Board of Education, but the Democrat controlled legislature and governor would not fund so that these schools for primarily black and Hispanic students could open. One of those was the Danbury Prospect Charter School, which had been approved by the State Board of Education in October 2018. Danbury Prospect Charter School even announced in 2021 that it had a twenty-five-million-dollar pledge from an anonymous philanthropist toward building the (grades sixth to twelfth) school. Nonetheless, even the local Democrat state representatives continued to oppose funding of this school for primarily Hispanic and black students lest one dollar of funding for the public school monopoly be jeopardized. That qualifies as "progressive" politics in Connecticut. The state over the citizen.[143]

The last thing that should be done is that the failed model in Connecticut should be promoted. But that is what the public school monopoly did. President Joseph Biden nominated then-Commissioner Cardona for Secretary of Education for the United States of America in December 2020. Secretary Cardona was sworn in on

---

[143] Thalheim, Peter, *Connecticut, Formerly the Constitution State: How the Politicians and Judges Have Subjected the Citizen to the State* (Page Publishing: Conneaut Lake), 2021.

March 2, 2021. Thus, the leader of a statewide school system that has failed high needs students and a teacher union and statist system that have fought tooth and nail against school choice for high needs—black, white, Hispanic, Asian, and other students—was promoted. And the reader wonders why the performance of black and Hispanic students continues to lag, not just in Connecticut, but nationwide? Some of the highest performing public schools in the states of New York and Connecticut are public charter schools peopled by high needs black, Hispanic, white, Asian, and other students!

The indictment against the opponents of school choice should be unsealed and filed.

Chapter 22

Structural Racism/Statism as Practiced by the Teachers Unions

WHAT PART DOES structural racism play here? Centrally. What is structural racism? It is important that you physically write down what you think "structural racism" is. "Structural racism" became a catch-all phrase in the aftermath of the killing of George Floyd in May 2020 to indicate that a citizen was against something, and the citizen was not complicit in the system that allowed "structural racism" to exist. But asking someone what "structural racism" is can produce almost as many answers as when one hundred economists are asked the best way to grow the economy. For that reason, it would be helpful if the reader would jot down on a piece of paper or in their cell phone what they believe "structural racism" to be.

The expression "structural racism" received frequent mentions in protests, in newspapers, on television, and on social media platforms, but there is no generally agreed definition of what "structural racism" is. It is argued here that structural racism overlaps greatly with structural statism, which are the obstacles that the statists put in the way of the citizen to go to school, to acquire shelter, get a job, hold a job, work, pay for necessities, pay for utilities, etc. It is the hurdles, burdens, and barriers that the state puts in your way to earn your keep, to learn, to put a roof over your family's head, to put food on your plate, and to pursue happiness as you see fit. If you support a proactive strong government, chances are you have fortified structural statism/racism to make it more difficult for your fellow citizens, in general, and blacks, in particular, to earn his or her living and make it forward in life.

If you made a Venn diagram of two overlapping circles, and in one circle, you wrote what comprises structural racism and in the other circle you wrote what comprises structural statism of the hurdles, burdens, and barriers that the state puts in the way of blacks in America, the vast majority of the two circles would overlap each other. Ergo, what comprises structural racism comprises structural statism.

Have your past political choices supported or enabled "structural racism?" Though pure of heart, can you entertain the possibility that your reflexive policy choices seemed logical and benevolent but ended up doing the opposite of what you intended? Will you continue to make the same political choices to support and enable "structural racism?" Many whites believe that they have not consciously abetted what could be characterized as structural racism and that if their past choices had abetted structural racism that they would not repeat the same mistake twice. Getting up on a soapbox to tell the world that you will fight to make a better world does not get us far if you merely double down on failed policies of the past, ambivalent to the unintended consequences of your choices, such as your support of the AFT, NEA, and their affiliates to defame and block school choice for high-needs students. Can the citizen consider that what they supported before, although done with good intentions, may have abetted structural racism?

Are you a chief executive officer of a corporation or public entity and use that position to issue statements to accentuate your enlightenment and how you are going to lead your company and the nation to a better place? Can you accept that you haven't a clue and that you are likely to double down on the ruinous policies that you had supported in the past? This is not focused on how you have handled your business but on your political choices. That is the definition of insanity by doing the same thing over and over again and expecting a different result.

When the government policies and laws that a chief executive officer of a corporation or public entity has supported in the past may have strengthened the "structural racism" of the NEA, AFT, and their affiliates to block school choice for high-needs black, Hispanic, Asian and other communities of color, more of the same will not change the outcome, even when you promise more funding to do more of the same but block school choice and vouchers.

Are you like our betters who have higher educational degrees or higher financial net worth, who think they are so smart and clairvoyant as to deny these parents and guardians their choice? The statists don't know these children like their parents and guardians. Would you make a different choice for your own children if you were offered the choice of a public charter school or vouchers for a private school versus a local public school that was consistently failing the math and English standardized tests of your state? Will you continue to deny these children school choice in the aftermath of the killing of George Floyd?

Of those opposed to school choice, some are bigots who dislike anything having to do with religion. Is that you? Others will say that the state should not give any money to a religious school. But this is cutting off our nose to spite our face. The religious schools achieve higher results in math, English, and post-secondary school studies. Would it be okay to give vouchers for high-needs students to attend a nonreligious school? Would you deny another high-needs student the road to success that Justice Sotomayor traveled from public housing via a Catholic private school?

Do you fancy yourself better than the parents and guardians of African-American and Hispanic students? As shared above, the opponents of school choice use various rationales to argue against school choice for these parents and guardians. But once the parents and guardians have made their choice, it is no longer time for the opponents to question the choice of the parents and guardians. These parents and guardians are with their children all the time. They know their children. You do not. You cannot prejudge their children and decide that they should not have the opportunity to attend a public charter or private school with the help of a voucher.

The protests after the killing of George Floyd and Breonna Taylor as well as the Covid-19 pandemic have shown that the two largest teachers' unions, the NEA, and the AFT are a king with no clothes as they gleefully work against public charter schools for African-American, Hispanic, white, Asian, and other students from high-needs environments, and, as required by law, they promote first, their teachers; second, themselves; and third, our children. And while they may have no clothes, they have plenty of muscle to intimidate and vilify any opponent of their aggrandizement along with the state. Who will speak up for our children, black and white, if the NEA and AFT, with the local Parent Teacher's Associations as their lackeys, promote the agenda of the NEA and AFT against school choice? Will you speak up for our children and their parents and guardians' right to choose?

Consider the headlines in 2020 after the Covid-19 coronavirus shut down schools and news outlets decried the disparate impact of stay-at-home schooling for black and Hispanic students. Students from poorer socioeconomic backgrounds did not have the laptops, neither the Internet connections, nor a quiet space to participate in online learning that their better-off peers had. There were stories that black and Hispanic students were falling further behind with remote learning during the Covid-19 pandemic. That is wrong. Countries such as Holland, Sweden, Germany, China, and Australia had reopened their schools. There is data that Covid-19 is much less lethal to children than adults. There is risk, and the risk-averse media will tell the story of this and that young person who died from Covid-19.

In previous years, they did not tell stories of young people, middle-aged people, or of senior citizens who died of the seasonal flu, and tens of thousands do die each year of the flu. In the summer of 2020, the teachers' unions in the United States weighed in against reopening in the fall as there was too much risk. They were correct that there were more risks for the entire staff of teachers, administrators, janitors, kitchen workers, etc. But how were these other countries able to put the interest of their children first and we were not able to? How is it that public unions were offered vaccinations against the Covid-19 virus in the field of education in exchange for opening K-6 schooling shortly after, but the public unions were reticent whilst our children fell further behind? Our children should be first and not third!

Conclusion

THE OPPOSITION OF the AFT and NEA to public charter schools and school choice for black, Hispanic, Asian, white, and other children from high-needs communities is the epitome of power politics. It is a fight of adults against children, and that is never a fair fight. Just the expression of a choice by the parents and guardians of these children should end the matter, and the way should be made clear for school choice, public charters, and vouchers. The AFT and NEA want to fight these parents and guardians all the way. The statists have maliciously used the COVID-19 pandemic of 2020 to restrict and undermine public charter schools as well as private schools in the hope of reducing their student bodies or eliminating them altogether, thereby maintaining a public school monopoly. George Wallace, who stood in the doors of the University of Alabama to bar the entry of African American students, would be proud of the AFT and NEA for standing in the door of public charter schools telling African American, Hispanic, Asian, white, and other students from high-needs environments that they cannot enter! That is a sad legacy for the AFT and the NEA despite their protestations that they are progressives or that they fight for the underserved. There are countless individual teachers who are members of the AFT and NEA who do heroic and selfless work every day to help our students get a good education, but that does not excuse the machinations of the AFT and NEA against our children, public charter schools, vouchers, and school choice. The school-to-prison pipeline goes through their headquarters as the students attending public charter schools and religious and non-religious private schools through vouchers are far less likely to end up in prison. That is the science. That is the math. That is the data. Let the parents decide. Let the guardians decide. Let our children and young people have a choice. If your parents had a choice of where to send you as a child or you had a choice of where to send your children, why would you deny school choice to black, Hispanic, Asian, white, and other American children from high-needs communities?

PART 1: SCHOOL INFORMATION AND EXECUTIVE SUMMARY

Name of Charter School:	Year School Opened:
Stamford Charter School for Excellence	2015
Street Address:	City/Zip Code:
1 Schuyler Avenue	Stamford, CT 06902
School Director:	School Director Contact Information:
Kevin Fischer	KFischer@stamfordexcellence.org/203 989-0000
Grades Authorized to Serve in 2019-20:	Charter Term:
PK-5	2015-2020

1. **School Performance Best Practices:** In 250 words or less, summarize a successful school model resulting in strong student outcomes and a positive school climate during the 2018-19 school year. Describe the strategy and its impact on the school referencing quantitative data. Provide evidence of collaboration with local school districts in this area, as appropriate.

Stamford Charter School for Excellence (SCSE, Stamford Excellence) is in its fifth year of operation, serving scholars in grades PK-5. Stamford Excellence utilizes a holistic approach to cultivate lifelong scholars equipped with the skills, knowledge, and habits for success in high school, college, and chosen careers. Our twelve key design elements summate the school's model and serve as the cornerstones of our quality instructional program. Our model is designed specifically to address the individualized needs of every student and promote maximum achievement through collaborative and data-driven instruction. We offer courses in the core subjects of language arts, mathematics, social studies, and science, as well as art, music, computer science, and physical education.

One distinguishing feature of Stamford Excellence is our grade cohort model. While each grade level teacher is assigned a classroom of students, all teachers on a grade level are responsible for the learning of all students across the grade. Flexible instructional groupings uniquely tailored for every child's needs are availed daily and based on ongoing real-time data. Teachers monitor student progress through a robust assessment model to offer highly supportive and differentiated instruction that targets the needs of students.

During the 2018-19 school year, an aggregate 90% of our scholars attained proficiency on state exams. Our parents were engaged in a variety of activities including concerts, curriculum nights, and our charter renewal public hearing. We attribute our outcomes to the hard work of our scholars and staff, our partnership with families, and our adherence to our school model that promotes collaborative, data-driven, differentiated instruction.

PART 2: SCHOOL PERFORMANCE

2. **School Goals:** State the school's mission statement. Provide the school's mission-specific, measurable goals. Analyze school progress toward these goals, providing data as appropriate. Add/Remove rows, as necessary.

Mission Statement:
The mission of the Stamford Charter School for Excellence is to prepare young people from Stamford to compete for admission to and succeed in top public, private and parochial high schools by cultivating their intellectual, artistic, social, emotional and ethical development. The school will accomplish this by offering a challenging and rigorous academic curriculum, which at the earliest of grades will have an eye towards college preparation. To achieve this, we will create a supportive and caring environment that at all times maintains high expectations of our students.

Goal Statement:	Evidence of Progress toward Goal:
Students will demonstrate adequate achievement throughout the school year in preparation to meeting and exceeding college and career readiness objectives as measured by statewide assessments.	SCSE utilizes the F&P to measure growth in literacy skills, Curriculum Based Assessments to monitor progress towards mathematical skill acquisition, and ICAs at testing grades to measure progress towards mastery of standards. The school also administers the Measures of Academic Progress (MAP). (See Student Achievement Data Tables).
75% of the students in third and fourth grade will score proficient on the SBAC exam in ELA and Math.	Our scholars scored 85% proficient on SBAC ELA and 95% on SBAC Math. Combined ELA and Math district scores resulted in SCSE being ranked 1st in the state at 90%.
The school will advance scholarly achievement by creating a culture of positive work habits, safe and appropriate conduct, and opportunities for healthy social-emotional interactions. Students will demonstrate character virtues summarized by the acronym, "RISE UP" (Responsibility, Integrity, Success, Etiquette, Unity, and Pride) and our core values of Respect, Citizenship, Teamwork, and Honesty with a College-Bound Attitude.	SCSE utilizes a variety of measures and means to build and monitor character development. Student performance towards these measures is monitored and analyzed through attendance and tardiness, discipline referrals, and suspension rates. As indicated in the table below, Stamford Excellence has maintained average daily attendance rates above 95% each year. Our absenteeism rate rose in 2017-18, which we attribute to high incidences of illness and inclement weather, as well as a number of families who were forced to return to their native countries to renew their green cards. Our efforts to mitigate resulted in a decline by 2018-19. We continue to educate our scholars on strategies such as hand hygiene to prevent the spread of illness, and educate our families on the importance of attending school daily in a timely manner. Our suspension rates also declined in 2018-19, and our expulsion rate remained at zero. We continue to build and monitor character development in the classrooms and utilize school-wide behavior management programs to teach essential skills, habits, and positive attitudes for success.

*Source: CSDE analysis based on district submitted and certified data.

need to help students achieve greater success.

The progression of our scholars throughout the school year in preparation for meeting and exceeding college and career readiness objectives as measured by statewide examinations is perhaps most clearly illustrated in Tables A.10 and A.11, which shows leveled performance from the first administration of the ICA in December (ICA1) to the SBAC exams in May. Table A.10 shows performance level migration for the ELA exam. For example, 25 scholars tested at a level 1 for ICA1. By the second administration in March (ICA2), nine of those original 25 scored a level 1, twelve scored a level 2, and three scored a level 3. By the third ICA administration in May (ICA3), five scored a level 1, twelve scored a level 2, six scored a level three and two achieved a level 4. By the time the scholars reached the state exam, nine scored a level 2, seven scored a level 3, and nine scored a level 4. As a result of the data-based instruction, interventions and remediation implemented routinely at Stamford Excellence, 100% of our scholars who originally scored a level 1 advanced, and 72% reached proficiency and above. In math, of the 12 scholars who tested at a level 1 on ICA1, 100% reached a higher level by the state exam, and all but 1 student tested proficient.

As seen in Tables A.1 and A.2, in our inaugural year of state testing, our third grade scholars achieved 81.6% proficiency in ELA, compared to 48.4% by the district, and 55.3% by the state of Connecticut. In math, 93.9% of our scholars achieved proficiency, compared to 41.8% by the district, and 46.8% by the state. Our aggregate scores made Stamford Excellence the second highest performing 'district' in the state overall. Additionally, 44.9% of our scholars achieved a level 4 in ELA, and 61.2% achieved a level 4 in Math (Table A.3). Moreover, our average scale scores for both third grade ELA and Math fell within the proficiency ranges of fourth graders (Tables A.5 and A.6). Stamford Excellence also attained an accountability index of 94.5, which garnered the school the classification of a 2017-18 School of Distinction for High Performance.

In 2018-19, 85.7% of our third and fourth grade scholars achieved proficiency in ELA, compared to 47.8% by the district and 55.7% for the state. In math, 94.9% of our scholars achieved proficiency, compared to the district's 42.8% and 48.1% for the state. As shown in Table A.4, we see again that the greater majority of our scholars attained a level 4, illustrating that our scholars are meeting and exceeding grade level expectations. Similarly in Tables A.5 and A.6, we see that our scholars' average scale scores fell within the proficiency ranges of the subsequent grade levels.

Student Achievement Data Tables

TABLE A.1

2017-18 SBAC ELA and Math Exams Performance[1] (% Levels 3 & 4) and Statewide Comparisons[2]							
Subject Grade	ELA 3	ELA 4	ELA 5	ELA 6	ELA 7	ELA 8	ELA 3-8
Stamford Excellence	81.6	N/A	N/A	N/A	N/A	N/A	81.6
Stamford Public Schools	47.1	46.4	55.5	46.0	46.9	47.5	48.4
All CT Charter Schools							44.9
All CT Host Districts							32.9
All CT Public Schools	53.1	54.9	58.4	54.3	55.0	56.1	55.3
Subject Grade	Math 3	Math 4	Math 5	Math 6	Math 7	Math 8	Math 3-8
Stamford Excellence	93.9	N/A	N/A	N/A	N/A	N/A	93.9
Stamford Public Schools	47.1	48.8	44.1	35.1	38.2	36.4	41.8
All CT Charter Schools							37.1
All CT Host Districts							24.4
All CT Public Schools	53.8	51.3	45.0	43.9	44.1	43.0	46.8

---

[1] Data retrieved from: http://edsight.ct.gov/SASPortal/main.do
[2] Northeast Charter Schools Network. Retrieved from http://www.nccharters.org/state_testing_data

TABLE A.2

2018-19 SBAC ELA and Math Exams Performance (% Levels 3 & 4) and Statewide Comparisons

Subject Grade	ELA 3	ELA 4	ELA 5	ELA 6	ELA 7	ELA 8	ELA 3-8
Stamford Excellence	87.8	83.6	N/A	N/A	N/A	N/A	85.7
Stamford Public Schools	48.9	46.9	50.4	48.3	45.3	46.9	47.8
All CT Charter Schools							43.7
All CT Host Districts							27.4
All CT Public Schools	54.3	54.6	58.1	55.3	56.1	55.8	55.7
Subject Grade	**Math 3**	**Math 4**	**Math 5**	**Math 6**	**Math 7**	**Math 8**	**Math 3-8**
Stamford Excellence	100	89.8	N/A	N/A	N/A	N/A	94.9
Stamford Public Schools	51.8	48.2	43.7	38.7	38.4	35.0	42.8
All CT Charter Schools							34.0
All CT Host Districts							15.7
All CT Public Schools	55.0	52.5	46.5	45.4	46.1	43.5	48.1

TABLE A.3

Stamford Excellence, Stamford School District (SSD), and CT Test Performance - % At Each Level[3]

YEAR	ELA					MATH				
2017-18	SCSE Gr 3	SSD Gr 3	SSD 3-8	CT Gr 3	CT 3-8	SCSE Gr 3	SSD Gr 3	SSD 3-8	CT Gr 3	CT 3-8
% Level 1	-	27.5	27.7	23.7	23.5	-	26	31.6	24	27.8
% Level 2	-	25.4	23.9	23.2	21.2	-	26.9	26.6	22.3	25.5
% Level 3	36.7	23.9	28.5	23.4	30.3	32.7	26.8	20.9	28.9	23.1
% Level 4	44.9	23.2	19.9	29.7	25	61.2	20.2	20.9	24.8	23.6
% Level 3 & 4	81.6	47.1	48.4	53.1	55.3	93.9	47.1	41.8	53.8	46.8

TABLE A.4

Stamford Excellence, Stamford School District (SSD), and CT Test Performance - % At Each Level[4]

YEAR	ELA						MATH					
2018-19	SCSE Gr 3	SCSE Gr 4	SSD Gr 3	SSD Gr 4	CT Gr 3	CT Gr 4	SCSE Gr 3	SCSE Gr 4	SSD Gr 3	SSD Gr 4	CT Gr 3	CT Gr 4
% Level 1	-	-	26.3	30.7	23.5	27.8	-	-	25.2	23.4	23.6	20.0
% Level 2	12.2	16.3	24.8	22.4	22.3	17.6	-	10.2	23.0	28.3	21.4	27.5
% Level 3	14.3	26.5	22.9	22.9	23.4	22.9	34.7	34.7	28.9	27.5	29.0	27.4
% Level 4	73.5	57.1	26.0	24.0	30.9	31.7	65.3	55.1	22.9	20.7	26.1	25.0
% Level 3 & 4	87.8	83.6	48.9	46.9	54.3	54.6	100	89.8	51.8	48.2	55.0	52.5

TABLE A.5

Stamford Excellence, Stamford School District (SSD), and CT Test Performance – Average Scale Scores[5]

YEAR	ELA						MATH					
	SCSE Gr 3	SCSE Gr 4	SSD Gr 3	SSD Gr 4	CT Gr 3	CT Gr 4	SCSE Gr 3	SCSE Gr 4	SSD Gr 3	SSD Gr 4	CT Gr 3	CT Gr 4
2017-18	2484	N/A	2422	N/A	2435	N/A	2520	N/A	2432	N/A	2440	N/A
2018-19	2520	2547	2426	2463	2437	2478	2530	2557	2437	2476	2443	2486

[3] Data retrieved from: http://edsight.ct.gov/SASPortal/main.do
[4] Data retrieved from: http://edsight.ct.gov/SASPortal/main.do
[5] Data retrieved from: http://edsight.ct.gov/SASPortal/main.do

CT SBAC SCALE SCORE RANGES						
ELA/Literacy	Grade 3	Grade 4	Grade 5	Grade 6	Grade 7	Grade 8
Level 4	2490-2623	2533-2663	2582-2701	2618-2724	2649-2745	2668-2769
Level 3	2432-2489	2473-2532	2502-2581	2531-2617	2552-2648	2567-2667
Level 2	2367-2431	2416-2472	2442-2501	2457-2530	2479-2551	2487-2566
Level 1	2114-2366	2131-2415	2201-2441	2210-2456	2258-2478	2288-2486
Mathematics	Grade 3	Grade 4	Grade 5	Grade 6	Grade 7	Grade 8
Level 4	2501-2621	2549-2659	2579-2700	2610-2748	2635-2778	2653-2802
Level 3	2436-2500	2485-2548	2528-2578	2552-2609	2567-2634	2586-2652
Level 2	2381-2435	2411-2484	2455-2527	2473-2551	2484-2566	2504-2585
Level 1	2189-2380	2204-2410	2219-2454	2235-2472	2250-2483	2265-2503

Tables A.7 through A.9 illustrate the performance of our subgroups in comparison to peers attending other schools in the district and state. As indicated, a significantly higher percentage of our scholars are testing proficient on state exams. Additionally, the gap between subgroup performance and that of the aggregate are significantly lower, thereby illustrating our ability to close historical achievement gaps.

TABLE A.7

	SCSE 2017-18		SCSE 2018-19		SSD 17-18		CT 17-18	
2018 and 2019 SBAC ELA & MATH RESULTS BY GRADE AND SUBGROUP COMPARISONS SCSE, STAMFORD SCHOOL DISTRICT (SSD), AND STATE[6]								
	ELA	MATH	ELA	MATH	ELA	MATH	ELA	MATH
GRADE/SUBGROUP	% Levels 3 & 4	% Levels 3 & 4	% Levels 3 & 4	% Levels 3 & 4	% Levels 3 & 4	% Levels 3 & 4	% Levels 3 & 4	% Levels 3 & 4
Grade 3	81.6	93.9	88.2	100	47.1	47.1	53.1	53.8
Grade 4	N/A	N/A	82.4	90.2	46.4	48.8	54.9	51.3
Grade 5	N/A	N/A	N/A	N/A	55.5	44.1	58.4	45.0
Grade 6	N/A	N/A	N/A	N/A	46.0	35.1	54.3	43.9
Grade 7	N/A	N/A	N/A	N/A	46.9	38.2	55.0	44.1
Grade 8	N/A	N/A	N/A	N/A	47.5	36.4	56.1	43.0
Grades 3-8	81.6	93.9	85.3	95.1	48.4	41.8	55.3	46.8
American Indian/ Alaskan	-	-	-	-	-	-	44.7	35.3
Asian	100	100	100	100	76.4	73.3	76.1	75.0
Black/African American	83.3	91.7	77.1	89.6	31.3	20.5	33.2	21.7
Hispanic/Latino	73.3	100	87.1	100	35.3	28.9	34.1	25.3
Native Hawaiian/ Pacific Islander	-	-	-	-	-	-	54.3	44.9
Multiracial	0*	0*	-	-	57.3	46.2	58.7	49.0
White	-	-	-	-	69.8	64.8	68.7	60.4

[6] Data retrieved from: http://edsight.ct.gov/SASPortal/main.do

Students With Disabilities	60	80	45.5	100	8.8	7.4	16.2	11.7
FRPL	81.1	91.9	80.3	92.4	33.7	26.8	35.1	25.8
ELL	100*	100*	100	100	7.2	8.5	12.1	12.8

* Denotes 1 student in group

TABLE A.8[7]

2017-18 SBAC EXAM – DISAGGREGATED BY GRADE AND SUBGROUP - % At/Above Proficient[7]

	Gr.	SCSE						STAMFORD PUBLIC SCHOOLS						CT					
		All	Black/African American	Hispanic	FRPL	ELL	SWD	All	Black/African American	Hispanic	FRPL	ELL	SWD	All	Black/African American	Hispanic	FRPL	ELL	SWD
ELA	3	81.6	83.3	73.3	81.1	100	60	47.1	28.1	31.5	31.3	9.4	9.7	53.1	33.0	32.3	33.5	17.9	16.1
	4	-	-	-	-	-	-	46.4	27.3	35.2	32.9	13.9	8.8	54.9	33.7	34.9	35.7	18.1	17.2
	5	-	-	-	-	-	-	55.5	45.4	41.8	41.8	10.7	10.8	58.4	36.2	38.2	38.4	12.8	18.0
	6	-	-	-	-	-	-	46.0	28.7	33.3	30.6	-	5.0	54.3	31.9	32.2	33.6	5.6	15.1
	7	-	-	-	-	-	-	46.9	29	35.5	31.9	-	9.1	55.0	31.2	33.0	33.6	5.5	14.8
	8	-	-	-	-	-	-	47.5	28	33.7	32.3	-	9.9	56.1	33.2	33.9	35.3	4.5	16.0
	3-8	81.6	83.3	73.3	81.1	100	60	48.4	31.3	35.3	33.7	7.2	8.8	55.3	33.2	34.1	35.1	12.1	16.2
MATH	3	93.9	91.7	100	91.9	100	80	47.1	23.6	34.7	31.8	12.6	13.9	53.8	30.3	32.6	33.5	23.7	18.2
	4	-	-	-	-	-	-	48.8	24.4	37.9	35.1	18.4	9.5	51.3	26.3	30.3	30.9	18.6	15.6
	5	-	-	-	-	-	-	44.1	26.7	31.3	29.2	9.6	5.7	45.0	18.9	24.4	24.3	9.3	11.3
	6	-	-	-	-	-	-	35.1	13.4	22.0	20.1	-	4.4	43.9	19.2	22.3	22.4	5.1	8.9
	7	-	-	-	-	-	-	38.2	16.9	25.4	22.0	-	4.9	44.1	18.3	21.5	21.9	5.4	9.1
	8	-	-	-	-	-	-	36.4	17.5	20.6	20.6	-	6.3	43.0	17.7	19.7	21.2	4.1	8.4
	3-8	93.9	91.7	100	91.9	100	80	41.8	20.5	28.9	26.8	8.5	7.4	46.8	21.7	25.3	25.8	12.8	11.7

TABLE A.9[8]

2018-19 SBAC EXAM – DISAGGREGATED BY GRADE AND SUBGROUP - % At/Above Proficient[8]

	Gr.	SCSE						STAMFORD PUBLIC SCHOOLS						CT					
		All	Black/African American	Hispanic	FRPL	ELL	SWD	All	Black/African American	Hispanic	FRPL	ELL	SWD	All	Black/African American	Hispanic	FRPL	ELL	SWD
ELA	3	88.2	80.0	93.3	87.5	100	66.7	48.9	34.1	42.5	35.4	16.4	16.7	54.3	34.2	35.5	36.1	22.2	18.2
	4	82.4	73.9	81.3	73.5	100	20.0	46.9	26.1	36.8	32.4	15.4	8.1	54.6	33.6	34.7	36.2	17.9	17.4
	5	-	-	-	-	-	-	50.4	30.3	38.2	37.4	9.9	9.8	58.1	35.9	38.3	39.6	14.1	17.7
	6	-	-	-	-	-	-	48.3	31.9	39.2	34.1	3.9	7.0	55.3	34.4	35.3	36.1	6.7	15.4
	7	-	-	-	-	-	-	45.3	27.5	35.3	29.7	-	6.2	56.1	33.4	35.7	37.1	6.1	17.0
	8	-	-	-	-	-	-	46.9	28.3	37.7	34.3	-	8.3	55.8	33.6	34.4	36.2	3.1	15.6
	3-8	85.3	77.1	87.1	80.3	100	45.5	47.8	29.6	38.3	33.9	9.1	9.3	55.7	34.2	35.7	36.9	13.4	16.9
MATH	3	100	100	100	100	100	100	51.8	28.5	45.5	38.1	24.9	17.8	55.0	31.2	35.2	35.7	27.6	18.6
	4	90.2	78.3	100	85.3	100	100	48.2	22.0	39.5	33.7	19.7	9.5	52.5	27.8	31.4	32.8	20.5	16.9
	5	-	-	-	-	-	-	43.7	19.7	33.2	30.2	11.0	4.6	46.5	20.5	26.6	27.2	12.7	11.8
	6	-	-	-	-	-	-	38.7	20.1	26.9	23.6	-	-	45.4	21.9	24.5	24.8	5.8	9.6
	7	-	-	-	-	-	-	38.4	17.6	27.2	23.0	-	4.5	46.1	20.4	23.6	25.0	5.4	10.9
	8	-	-	-	-	-	-	35.0	14.7	26.2	21.7	-	-	43.5	18.6	20.7	21.2	3.4	8.3
	3-8	95.1	89.6	100	92.4	100	100	42.8	20.3	33.1	28.5	11.2	7.2	48.1	23.3	27.0	27.9	14.7	12.6

---

[7] Data retrieved from: http://edsight.ct.gov/SASPortal/main.do

[8] Data retrieved from: http://edsight.ct.gov/SASPortal/main.do

PART 4: STUDENT POPULATION

10. Enrollment and Demographic Data: Provide 2018-19 student demographic and enrollment information.

Grades Served:			PK, K, 1, 2, 3, 4		Student Enrollment:				320					
% Free/Reduced-Price Lunch:			48%		% Black:				49.7%					
% Special Education:			5.6%		% Hispanic:				22.2%					
% Limited English Proficiency:			10.9%		% Caucasian:				.09%					

2018-19 Enrollment by Grade Level:

PK	K	1	2	3	4	5	6	7	8	9	10	11	12	Total
59	53	54	53	50	51									**320**

11. Enrollment Efforts: Summarize the school's efforts to attract, enroll, and retain a diverse and representative student population, including minority students, low-income students, English learners, and students with disabilities.

Pursuant to the Connecticut General Statutes (C.G.S.) Section 10-15c, SCSE maintains an open enrollment policy and does not discriminate on the basis of race, ethnicity, sex, gender identity, religion, disability, national origin, native language, or sexual orientation. Although the school typically appeals to families and populations in high-needs communities that have been traditionally underserved, the school does not enact enrollment preferences beyond currently enrolled students and siblings of enrolled scholars. SCSE accepts applications from legal guardians of all age and grade eligible students. Applications are provided in English and Spanish, and available for translation online to the prevailing languages of the community. Enrollment is determined by a blind lottery. The school accepts completed applications from mid-January through April 1 for the lottery, and on a rolling basis for our waiting list. Applications are submitted electronically through the school's website, or in hard copy. Once all vacancies are filled through the lottery, the waiting list is created. Applicants who have siblings already attending the school are given preference for any vacancies that occur during the school year. Enrollment packets clearly articulate the documentation that must be submitted, to include appropriate proofs of identification, residency, and health records.

The school deliberately extends its outreach efforts in high needs communities to attract and retain a diverse student body that is reflective of the community it serves, to include comparable or greater enrollment of special populations including minority students, low-income students, English Language Learners, and students with disabilities. SCSE utilizes a variety of strategies to attract a diverse student body with recruitment efforts, which include:

- Attendance and distribution of marketing materials at open houses, public meetings, meet-and-greets, and presentations at various community organizations such as preschools, daycare centers, head start programs, ESL programs for adults with school-aged children, county health centers, doctors' offices, libraries, family service providers, housing authorities and associations, counseling centers and support groups, tutoring groups, and places of worship (churches, mosques, temples, etc.)
- Neighborhood canvassing, especially in areas with higher concentrations of public housing developments and multicultural communities
- Distribution of flyers and mailings in English, Spanish, and prevailing languages
- Local media stations (radio and internet) that target both English and non-English speaking audiences

SCSE engages the community and hosts events such as open houses and meetings with the students, families, and community members. SCSE also includes bilingual staff members to support the recruiting efforts for families whose native language is one other than English.

Because we enroll scholars in grades PK and kindergarten, students of this age typically will not have extensive academic or behavioral records. Some students may have previously received early screening and interventions for academic, social, or behavioral difficulties. We continually emphasize to all families that the school's policies support open enrollment, non-discriminatory practices, and an inclusive educational model. Targeted outreach to specific populations such as families with children identified with special needs or English language learners receive more specific information about the programs and services that SCSE has to offer. Finally, the school ensures that comprehensive information is always available on the school's standing

By signing this Statement of Assurances on behalf of the Governing Board of **Stamford Charter School for Excellence**, I acknowledge that I understand the terms contained herein and affirm the validity of each statement to the best of my knowledge. I further understand that **Stamford Charter School for Excellence** may be subject to random audit by the CSDE to verify these statements.

Signature: _____

Name of Board Chairperson: _____Debra Logan-Rabb_____

Date: _____10/18/2019_____

About the Author

Peter Thalheim has brought his experience from sixty years of life starting as a two-year-old immigrant coming to America in 1963 to this book. He attended K-12 public school and obtained a bachelor's degree in European history and later a law degree. Admitted to the bars of the states of Connecticut and New York, he practiced commercial litigation, general corporate law, and residential real estate, amongst other matters. At the same time, he developed his skills as a home builder and contractor by doing some of the work with his own hands and back. He has traveled around the world, visiting the Soviet Union twice before it disappeared, and has visited Communist China three times in addition to his backpacking through Southeast Asia. He has also spent considerable time traveling and visiting in Europe, where he has employed his average knowledge of German, basic knowledge of French, and rudimentary knowledge of Russian to get about and converse. An enthusiastic American who loves the great outdoors, he has driven across the great country of the United States numerous times.

One of his proudest accomplishments was joining the United States Army Reserve as a JAG officer after starting work in New York City as a litigator. These years in the reserves shaped what would become Check "American!" More recently, Mr. Thalheim ran unsuccessfully for governor of the State of Connecticut in 2017–2018, which was inspired by the positive message of "Life, Love, Liberty" of Faith Tabernacle Missionary Baptist Church, an African American Baptist church in Stamford, Connecticut, that Mr. Thalheim regularly attends. During his campaign, Mr. Thalheim was introduced to the National Association for the Advancement of Colored People and has since been elected to the executive committee of the NAACP, Stamford, Connecticut, branch, in January 2020, a nonpartisan civil rights organization.

CPSIA information can be obtained
at www.ICGtesting.com
Printed in the USA
BVHW030333110422
633831BV00001B/3

9 781649 529954